Celebrating Curl
The Roarin' Game

Cameron McKiddie

First Published in Great Britain in 2009 by Cameron McKiddie

Copyright © Cameron McKiddie

Cameron McKiddie asserts the moral right to be identified as the author of this work

A catalogue record for this book is available from the British Library

ISBN-978-0-9563978-0-5

Printed and bound by Astute Scotland Ltd.
Silvie Way, Orchard Business Park,
Forfar.

Celebrating Curling –
The Roarin' Game

FOREWORD

Any person who takes on the task of producing a book on curling must appreciate the time and effort needed for research. Cameron has indeed carried out this work in a masterful way. "Celebrating Curling – The Roarin' Game" is at times a really humorous account of some curling events but also gives a factual knowledge, obviously done with some intense work. You will travel back through some of the great times in curling and I guarantee you will learn about curling people and events you have never heard about until now. The stories are all true!

Cameron, an Optometrist by profession, started curling in 1964 when he joined Kirriemuir Curling Club. He has always lived in Kirriemuir and became a "Made Curler" at the tender age of 26. He was a member of the Rotary Tour of Canada in 1984, thoroughly enjoying the camaraderie which only comes from a curling tour. Following in his father's footsteps he became President of his club in 1974 and again in 2008.

I am delighted Cameron has decided to take time to sit down and write this book and provide such an entertaining and inspiring celebration of the many things which make our game so special. I am sure this book will be enjoyed by curlers throughout the world and in the words of the Royal Caledonian Curling Club Constitution cannot be better described than "To unite curlers throughout the world into one Brotherhood of the Rink".

Bill Marshall,
President, Royal Caledonian Curling Club 2009-10

All proceeds from the sale of 'Celebrating Curling' will be used by Kirriemuir Curling Club for curling development and the encouragement and fostering of new participants, including juniors to this wonderful game.

Celebrating Curling

CONTENTS

The Roarin' Game

Note:
Curling is often called the Roaring Game from the sound produced from the stone travelling over the ice, more noticeable on outdoor ice as the noise echoes around the area.

Editors Note

When Kirriemuir Curling Club started plans to commemorate the Bicentenary of the Club's formation, I volunteered to produce a short history of the club. This record gleaned from minute books of the club would have been primarily of interest to Kirrie members themselves.

However my researches started to unearth a rich tapestry of poems, articles, stories and photographs of the grand game of curling and the special brotherhood surrounding it. Much agreeable and profitable time was spent reading through many old copies of the Annuals of the Royal Caledonian Curling Club, held in the archives of Kirriemuir Curling Club. Many of the poems and reports from the 'Annuals' are reprinted in these pages. Several months were spent in Kirriemuir library using microfilm to trawl through local newspaper reports on curling from the present day back to 1860. From many hundreds, I have selected only those where humour is paramount; those of particular significance in the annals of Kirriemuir Club and those wreathed in controversy. Of particular interest were curling reports of around the 1860's, which revealed a fascinating historical account of the life and, in particular, the language of those bygone years.

In 2006, a recorded interview with Kirrie Curling Club's oldest surviving past member, Wallace Neilson, then aged 91 gave a historical account of life and curling around Kirriemuir sixty and more years ago.

I soon realised that this treasure trove of material would have a much wider appeal to curlers the world over and perhaps even to 'nobodies'*

Assembling this material has been very much a labour of love and I hope readers will obtain as much enjoyment from this book as I had preparing it.

* One who has not been initiated into the Brotherhood of Curlers

Acknowledgements

I wish to pay tribute to those scribes of the past and present, both named and anonymous whose work appears in these pages. Could they have guessed that their sterling efforts would one day appear in print?

I wish to thank the Royal Caledonian Curling Club for granting permission to reproduce articles from the 'Annuals'. Thanks are also due to the publishers of the Kirriemuir Herald for allowing the 'curling reports' to be reproduced in this publication. To Roch Sullivan and Ross McMillan (Blue Jeans) of New Zealand, my thanks for supplying photographs and permitting reprints of poetry respectively.

Curling club member and award winning photographer Malcolm McBeath is not only responsible for some of the superb photography but also assisted in the preparation of 'Celebrating Curling'.

Kirriemuir artist Joyce Grubb whose painting of the last Grand Match appears on the front cover is also responsible for the beautiful illustrations, which appear in this book.

To all other contributors I give my thanks.

Dedication

To my wonderful wife Eunice, for her patience, encouragement and advice during the preparation of this book. Tragically, before this book was finished she contracted cancer and died on 14th August 2008.

Cameron McKiddie   22nd July 2009

Introduction

The Brotherhood of Curling

"Tae be guid friends alang life's road"

This line from the Curlers Grace* embodies the special bond that exists between curlers the world over. An affirmative reply to "Are you a curler?" is likely to elicit a warm smile of recognition and the strong hand of fellowship from those who share a love for the roarin' game. What grand it is to be a curler!

It would appear that this Brotherhood of Curling was forged way back in time and while there have been many changes in the game and indeed in life itself, the same bond is very much in evidence today. Each game still begins and ends with the hand of fellowship and whatever the result of the match, winning or losing on the ice is accepted in true sportsmanship.

The game itself will be contested vigorously in an effort to win but there is rarely much dissension, other than some gentle suggestions that maybe Lady Luck has helped the opposition or sotto voce that your own skip is not up to the mettle. Cheating, either deliberately or accidentally is so rare to be almost non-existent – few sports could compare to the fair play exhibited by curlers whatever their skill or position.

How did this integrity become established, apparently very early in the game's first tentative beginnings? Perhaps, as the game is thought to have started as a simple test between friends, neighbours and hamlets, the exponents already shared a mutual respect and liking through the close proximity of the community. Keen rivalries of course would have developed as they are today but an understanding of fairness and respect whatever their station within the community would have been the order of the day.

'Every man his name and surname'** – everyone was considered equal when they stepped onto the ice, be they landlord, laird, employer or employee and one progressed higher up the rink on ability only. While touching one's forelock was maybe the accepted deference in life at that time, this was not continued onto the ice.

This early establishment of fairness, respect and equality on the ice appears to have been passed down the generations of curlers and cemented into that special Brotherhood of the Rink.

By example and teaching, new curlers learn not only how to curl but soon understand the special relationship that curlers the world over enjoy.

So dear reader, be you a fellow curler or not, in this 'Celebration of Curling' you will find in verse, prose and reports, numerous examples of the Brotherhood of Curling ---

"Tae be guid friends alang life's road."

Full text – see page 100

**Said during the Curlers Court*

Celebrating Curling in Verse

These two poems embody the curlers' equality on the ice

Curling Toast

Fill up a bumper to the brim,
And let the toast go round
To Scotland's Curlers leal and true,
Wherever they are found;
Whether they dwell in lordly hall,
Or 'neath a roof of straw,
I ask not, but I ask of you
To pledge them ane and a'.
Well as the sportsman loves his gun
When once the frost sets in
If he's a curler *keen and clear*
It's never touched by him;

* broom

The bonspiel's now his only care
From morn till evening grey
Wi' well tied cowe* upon the ice,
He plays from day to day.
Both rich and poor, whenever met,
Enjoy alike the game;
Each strive to take the finest points,
And gather curling fame.
Then once again I ask of you,
To let the toast go round,
To Scotland's Curlers leal and true,
Whenever they are found.

BALFRON, 3d August 1874   R. Brown
RCCC Annual 1875

The King o' Games – 'The Curlin'

Come, brithers, join wi me and sing
In praise o' frosty days that bring
To high and low, to peasant, king,
The glorious joys o' curlin'.

It needna ane o' high degree
To be the chief around the tee;
The curler wha plays best – 'tis he
That skips the game o' curlin'.

See yonder lad, a country swain,
Wha lives his simple life alane,
Till John Frost claims him for his ain,
And forth he gangs a-curlin'. -

His mien* is bashfu' ; still you see
There is a fire intil his ee
That tells nor Duke nor Lord fears he
Whenever he gangs curlin'.

And tho' he's kent by only few,
Thae few ken weel what he can do.
And when he skips e'en a' maun* boo*,
For he's a King at curlin'.

He looks on curlers wi' disdain
Wha cry for licht or polished stane,
And swears that such should leave alane
The glorious game o' curlin'.

Auld Scotland, ye may weel be proud,
And sing their praises lang and loud,
The Channel Stanes – A' Curlers good –
The King o' Games – the Curlin'.

T.S.A (Waverley)
RCCC Annual 1893-4

*mien – appearance   *maun – must   * boo – bow

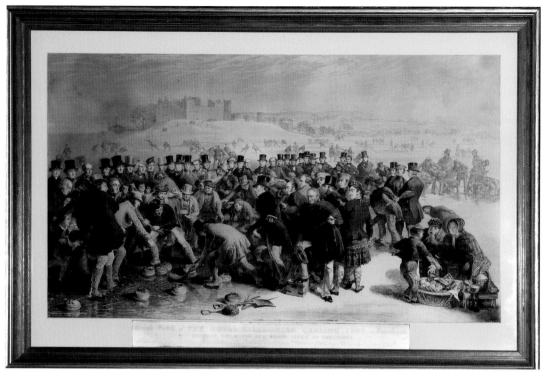

Every picture tells a story -1

Around August 1983, a Kirrie trio of Tom Somerville, Colin Smith and Cameron McKiddie had enjoyed a day at the golf links on the Old Course, St Andrews watching the final round of the Dunhill Cup. Afterwards they adjourned to the St Andrew's flat of Colin's friend Audrey. During a happy evening when drink was consumed, Colin suddenly turned to Audrey to say 'Cameron's into curling, he might be interested in taking away that big print you have lying in the hall'. The print was ushered through all 3½ft x 2½ft of it and to cut a long story short, Cameron arrived back in the wee hours, wakening his not amused wife to show what he had brought home from his day out at the Dunhill. It became a permanent feature in their dining room along with other curling memorabilia. However the story does not end quite yet. Attending the AGM of the Royal Caledonian Curling Club, held in Glenrothes in 2007, reference was made about a famous painting by Charles Lees, owned by the RCCC. This painting was not only costing the Club thousands to insure but also required cleaning at an estimated cost of £60,000+. Only then did Cameron realise that he had a print or possibly an engraving of this famous painting. Moreover on reading through old Annuals of the RCCC for material for this book, he came across not only a copy of the print but the legend putting a name to the RCCC officials pictured in the composite painting.

In that Annual of 1898, it is reported, that the original painting was purchased by one James Law of the Waverley Club for the grand sum of £116, 11s. and offered at that price to the RCCC who unanimously agreed to its purchase. It was noted that parts of the painting, which was by now 50 years old, were hard and dry and it was agreed to spend a *few pounds* to put it right.

The painting in oil by Charles Lees was completed in 1849 and depicted the Grand Match, which was held at Linlithgow Loch the previous year when 35 rinks from the North played 35 from the South. It was reported that with other unofficial games and spectators, around 6000 were present. The painting is 'Dedicated to the Office Bearers and Members of the Associated Clubs of the Royal Caledonian Curling Clubs.

At the AGM of 2007 the meeting agreed that the painting should be sold but only if it could be purchased by the National Gallery and remain in Scotland. Valued in excess of £500,000 it does require expensive renovation. It will be interesting to learn what eventually happens to this historical masterpiece.

'Now, what's my print worth?'   C.McKiddie

Press Reports

These have been selected for their historical curling significance, at times controversy and in particular their humour and arranged chronologically throughout this book.

Kirriemuir Observer 25th January 1862
AN OLD-TIME CURLERS' DINNER.

The annual dinner of the Kirriemuir Curling Club was held in Mitchelson's Commercial Hotel* on Monday last. Mr Gilruth, President of the Club, occupied the chair, supported on the right by Mr Forrest, Secretary, and on the left by the Rev. Mr Ramsay. Mr Mustard, Vice-president, did the duties of croupier. After doing ample justice to a "real curlers' dinner" of beef and greens, the cloth was removed. The chairman, after proposing the health of the Queen, the Prince of Wales, the other members of the Royal Family, then proposed "the Army, the Navy, and the Volunteers" coupling the toast with the name of Lieutenant Brodie. The toast was drunk amidst great cheering. Mr Brodie replied. The President then gave " The Royal Caledonian Curling Club" The toast was drunk with all the honours. Mr Forrest proposed the health of Captain Munro, the Patron of the Club. He said they were very much indebted to Captain Munro for the very handsome silver challenge cup(the cup was on the table), which he had been kind enough to present to the Club. The toast was drunk with great cheers. Mr Mustard proposed the Chaplain of the Club, Mr Ramsay returned thanks. Mr James Forrest proposed the health of Mr Osler, as the originator of the Club. Other toasts followed. The Club spent a happy evening, and, after paying a compliment to Mrs Mitchelson for the manner in which she had administered to their various wants, they separated, in the hope that "John Frost" would give them another opportunity of having a friendly contest this season.

* The Commercial Hotel was built in 1830, the only 4 storey building in Kirriemuir at that time, having a basement and a lift and situated at the corner of Bank Street and the High Street. It became known as Duncan's Corner when James Duncan established his grocery using the basement and ground floor. Floors above over the years have served as dentist and doctor's surgeries, and various offices and now mostly flats which are renowned for their sloping floors. The corner shop is presently unoccupied. Ed.

Kirriemuir Observer 23rd January 1864

On Monday the curlers dined together in Lennies* Hall. Mr Grant, contractor, presided and Mr Forrest acted as croupier. There was a large number of the Knights of the broom who did ample justice to mine host's excellent beef and greens, which they washed down with a flowing bowl of real Glenlivet. The court being formed, three candidates were initiated. The evening was then spent in toast, song and sentiment.

KIRRIEMUIR OBSERVER 13TH FEBRUARY 1864

The present severe frost had again allowed our curlers to enjoy their "roaring game". On Monday a match was played between the President and the Chaplain of the Club, for a quantity of meal for the industrious poor. The Chaplain beat the president by one point.

'COME TO MY KOWE'

A Lothian skip, directing one of his players of the name Bull, on one occasion created some amusement by saying: 'Bull, come to my kowe*.'

R.C.C.C. Annual 1926-27

* kowe or cowe – broom

* Lennies Hall called after the proprietor was part of the Railway Hotel – see page 13

My Ding-a-Ling

Tom* was Skip as smart as hell,
On his brush he hung a bell,
To lead Brian B* said here's this thing,
I want you to play on my ding-a-ling.

Chorus

My Ding-a-Ling, my Ding-a-Ling,
I want you to play on my Ding-a-Ling.
If curling is to mean a thing –
You must play on my Ding-a-Ling.

Jim Kelman had a stone to hide,
Threw the damn thing well outside.
He stood and blushed and then he cried,
Your Ding-a-Ling was far too wide.

Chorus

Danny Bell had to take the shot stone out,
He played and then we heard him shout,
That should make the old skip sing,
I've dropped it on his Ding-a-Ling.

Chorus

Skip Tom came up to play himself,
Threw the stone and then he fell,
His howling made the rafters ring,
The hack had caught his Ding-a-Ling.   C.McKiddie

* Tom Wakeford
* Brian Bonnyman
This was included in a toast to Forfar Curling Club in 1998, having been
adapted from a similar poem found in the files of Area 9 RCCC.
The poem is based on the Chuck Berry song of the same title.   Ed

Kirriemuir Observer 16th February 1864

On Tuesday a match between Kirriemuir and Coupar Angus and Kettins Curling Clubs came off on the Curling Pond at Glamis. The day was all that could be desired, and the ice in excellent condition. There was a good muster of both clubs, and a goodly number of spectators present. After a keen game the Coupar Angus and Kettins Club beat the opponents by 30 shots the members being :

Coupar Angus		Kirriemuir	
Mr. Jas Chalmers,	15	Mr Osler,	8
Mr John Watson	24	Mr Grant,	7
Mr D, Bett,	21	Dr Malloch,	15
	60		30

The medal was accordingly presented to Mr James Chalmers, President of Coupar Angus and Kettins Club. The two clubs afterwards dined together at the Glamis Hotel. Mr Grant, Kirriemuir occupied the chair, and Mr D.J. Bett discharged the duties of croupier. A substantial dinner in mine host's best style was served up, and discussed with keen appetites acquired during the competition. The cloth being removed, a pleasant evening was spent in true curler's style.

An Old Curler's Lament

1.
Though I'm just an old curler called Dudley,
Warm, gentle and sometimes quite cuddly,
Now I'm passed my prime,
I suppose it was time,
But I'd do it again, yes!, quite gladly.

2.
Having come north from out of the city,
Having lived here for years, it's a pity,
Though I drink quite a lot
Even more than a Scot,
I'm still known as the Ethnic Minority.

3.
On reaching my two score and ten,
I'm preaching my thoughts through my pen;
When I play the game,
It's never the same,
How I wish I was young once again.

4.
Old age treats you really quite tough,
When you find that you can't do your stuff.
When playing your guard,
You think it's quite hard,
Then you find that's it not hard enough.

5.
So you're there with your eye on the cup,
You try with a heave and a hup,
But though you may strain,
It's all been in vain,
When you find that you can't get it up.

6.
Hard stones may be fine in their way,
For knocking some guards quite astray,
But I feel more grand,
When with delicate hand,
I succeed with a tee perfect lay.

7.
But now I'm told, listen old pop,
The women they don't like to stop,
If you take the lead,
It's all that they need,
To ensure that they come out on top.

8.
But see here, my spirit's not doon
You'll see I'm still over the moon,
Though age be past middle,
I'm like an old fiddle,
Quite ready to play a new tune.   C. McKiddie

On the occasion of Kirrie Curler Dudley Dorman's
50th Birthday

Kirrie artist **Joyce Grubb** has captured a remarkable likeness of Dudley raising his glass

11

The Curlers' Court

In any publication about curling in Scotland, mention must be made of that long held tradition, the Curlers' Court, a feature of most Scottish clubs. It is as difficult to put an exact date on the instigation of courts as it is to decide when the game of curling first appeared but historical references suggests that some form of the game could have appeared as early as the 14th century.

'The Curlers Court, the origin of which was to punish petty offences committed on the ice and to initiate new members into the mysteries of Curling, appears to have been co-existent with Curling Clubs and Curling Brotherhoods, and to have been kept up by several clubs for well over 200 years.'

This much-used quotation in this case comes from the Constitution, Rules and Regulations, 1955 of the Angus Curling Province Royal Caledonian Curling Club. It has appeared in the same or similar vein in many other constitutions or publications of much earlier vintage.

In similar vein to that practised now, the Curlers Court would have fined members for petty offences committed on or off the ice and carried out in a tongue in cheek dignified but light heartened manner. It was also an occasion to initiate new curlers into the brotherhood of curlers and used by many clubs as a means of instructing new curlers into the methodology of the game. A feature of many clubs including my own was to instruct the newly made curlers into the various signs, instructions and etiquette of the game itself. However, having been fortified with Dutch courage beforehand; having come through the rigours of the 'making' and taken a celebratory drink or three afterwards, it is questionable how much of this imparted information would have been recalled the next morning.

In some clubs this tradition disappeared many years ago, in others it has been resurrected and for many it is a regular feature, sometimes annually, others less often and driven by the number of new curlers requiring to **be made**. As recent as the 1970's, in the Angus Province at least, only those who had been initiated

Pictured at Kirrie Curlers' Court in the Airlie Arms Hotel in 2005 are L-R, Carol Robbie, Alan Keillor(My Lord), Cameron McKiddie (My Lord's Officer), Jesma Lindsay & Peter Giles

into the brotherhood could play in open or inter-club competitions played under RCCC rules.

A made curler is one who has been through an initiation into the brotherhood of curlers, though nowadays we must add the sisterhood of curlers as many ladies clubs and mixed clubs will initiate both sexes into the mysteries of curling. Do the ladies receive the same treatment? – In this age of equality of the sexes – of course they do.

The Initiation ceremony can vary greatly from club to club but many clubs came to adopt much of the procedure as suggested in the constitution of the Grand Caledonian Curling Club formed in 1838. However there remains a great diversification of initiations, some favouring the traditional approach containing many similar aspects while others have developed their own peculiar rights of passage into the brotherhood. Over the past 40 years I have attended around 30 courts, mostly those of my own and neighbouring clubs, and have served as My Lord on a few occasions and My Lord's Officer in many more. During that time in my own club at least we have faithfully retained very similar traditional elements, which have some true relationship to the game. We ensure that every curler coming though their initiation is in safe hands and will never regret their right of passage. Heaven forbid that litigation be

Pictured at Kirrie Curlers' Court in the Airlie Arms Hotel in 2005 are L-R, newly made Brother of the Broom, Gerry Tierney being presented by Reporter Peter Giles

ever used as a result of inappropriate handling of an initiation.

The Editor, when aged 26 and a new curler was asked by the secretary of his Kirriemuir Club to represent Kirriemuir at a dinner to be held by Cortachy Curling Club at the Jubilee Arms Hotel, Dykehead. Anything for a free meal, he thought, and off he went like a lamb to slaughter, little knowing what was ahead of him as to his surprise and total ignorance, a court was fenced. One cannot of course reveal here the procedures of his making but three hours later, a wiser? and new made brother of the broom addressed the company on behalf of the newly made curlers. Does he still remember where he was made? "Oh Yes, and it wasn't at Cortachy!"

During my time as a member of Kirriemuir Club,

Courts have been held on average every three years and invariably the venue was either the Ogilvy Arms Hotel or Airlie Arms Hotel, until the closure of the former about 10 years ago. Many memorable courts were held and while it would be inappropriate to go into too much detail, the following examples of happenings are well remembered by those present.

As well as the customary goat, Kirrie club usually ensured that a member of the club who was a doctor was present. During the making of Ronnie Brown, 'the Dominie', the occasion proved too much for him and he fainted – fortunately the Doc, Big John Gilmour was on hand to ensure he was none he worse – having recovered sufficiently he was given a gentler passage to the end.

During his initiation 'The Grubber' lost his teeth – was he able to eat again?

Having come through most of his initiation 'Pots & Pans' his nickname for the evening was presented as a brother of the broom to 'My Lord' no less than five times before he was finally able to give the correct response to the 'words and counter words' . Yes, the reporter was suitably fined for his failure to properly prepare the candidate!

In 2005, at a crucial and dramatic stage of the making of Paddy Liddle, the room had grown quieter when the eerie silence was suddenly interrupted by the ringing of his mobile phone. It was his wife enquiring how he was getting on at his initiation! - - - -

Kirriemuir Observer 18th January 1865
"BEEF AND GREENS"

Monday last being "Auld Hansel Monday", the Kirriemuir Curling Club partook of their annual dinner of "beef and greens" in Mr Farquharson's Railway Hotel*. Mr Grant, C.E, President occupied the chair, while Mr Osler, representative member, officiated as croupier. After dinner, and the loyal toasts having been honoured, the Chairman proposed the toast of the evening "Prosperity to the Kirriemuir Curling Club" The health of their patron, Captain Munro, and other toasts followed. In proposing the health of their worthy chaplain, Rev. Mr Ramsay, the President remarked that he had no doubt many of the poor people were as anxious for "John Frost" as they – the curlers were, that they might partake of the boll of meal to be again played for between himself and the chaplain, and he hoped a larger stake would this year be made up by the other members of the Club so that the deserving poor might be all the better of their sport. A very pleasant evening was spent.

*Railway Hotel was situated in Bank Street on the west side of the Bank of Scotland. It eventually became Lowson's Garage and is now the Angus Council Access Office.

Perhaps topping them all is this report, which was recorded in 'Kirrie Life', published in 2001.

Flamin' Hell

There was panic at Kirrie Curlers Court

when during the makin' of a new curler,

his recoil from the 'Devil' momentary set

alight, first the floor, then a broom

followed by the ceiling.

The 'nobody' being made? – Watt Duncan –
Part Time Fireman

(Early 1980's – Ogilvy Arms Hotel)

Rouping the Stoup

Oh, what man could do with this rare stoup,

That time has come for me tae roup.

These coins an siller, man, they're heavy,

It's a' the fines from this court's levy.

There's unca there for nichts o' boozing,

Can you no' see, it's almost oozing.

My airms sae sair just haudin it up,

It's war than heavin' a muckle tup.

I'll gie it a shak, did ye hear that rattle

Come on then lads, are you ready for battle.

Some lad will win it but have nae fear,

By Christ it's fu, so it maun be dear.

C.McKiddie

Kirrie Curlers Court & others circa 1970

'Rouping the Stoup' – towards the end of the Court, fines which had been collected in the stoup, usually a metal jug or flagon were then auctioned (rouped) to the highest bidder.

"Now I want you to show me how well you deliver the stone" High jinks at Kirrie Curlers' Court, Airlie Arms Hotel 2005

To the Tune of 'Nobody's Child - By a newly made female at KCC Court 2005

1.
As we were quickly sweeping
A curling stone one day,
We sisters started speaking
Of the Curlers Court affray

2.
We heard of boisterous antics,
The firies were called out
The cauldron flames* had hit the roof,
Negligence, no doubt.

3.
My Lord had hit the whisky,
His officer in tow,
Both got a wee bit frisky,
So both are lying low.

4.
The floor, it got all slippy,
With water, ice and glar,
A Nobody had thrown a stone,
Both landed in the bar.

5.
The Nobodies in trauma,
Were pacified with gin,
Apparently they will not sue,
If we admit our sin.

6.
So the moral of this story,
For curlers far and wide
The Curlers Court is guid, guid fun,
When you use your wicked side.   *Carol Robbie*

* see 'Flamin' Hell' previous page

A curler does tend to remember their makin' at a Curlers' Court and the letter on the next page shows what a lasting impression it created for a visiting Canadian.

KIRRIEMUIR OBSERVER ......28TH JANUARY 1865

Thursday was a gala day for our curlers here, it being the day fixed upon to play for the elegant silver cup, presented to the club by Sir Thomas Munro, Bart, Lindertis, and which was gained last year by David Christison; as also for a very neat pair of curling stones, presented to the Club some years ago by James Forrest, Esq., banker, and which were held last year by Mr George Christison. The day, though dull, was sharp and bracing, and the ice keen, but not more than the curlers. At an early hour of the forenoon, about thirty curlers mustered, when the contest began, and was carried out with great spirit.

The utmost harmony prevailed, and after a close contest, in which some of the best play we have seen was displayed, Mr Osler of Glasswell was declared to be the winner of the cup, and Robert Forrest Esq., winner of the stones. In presenting the prizes Mr Grant, the President of the Club, congratulated the winners on the superior skill they had displayed on the ice that day, and expressed a hope that they would win them until they could keep and leave them as an heirloom to their families. A friendly match was then played by the members of the Club, at the close of which they adjourned to the Airlie Arms Hotel, where they were entertained by brothers Osler and Forrest, and spent a happy evening in draining the cup to the health of their highly respected brother who had that day carried it off.

Solid Silver Points Cup

Cup detail

Transcript of an interesting hand written letter from the KCC files

Winnipeg, Manitoba
Canada R3G 3B9
23rd February 1994

The Ancient Order of Curlers

Dear Sirs (Brethren actually as I am a member)

I have been meaning to write this letter for years but kept putting it off, etc, and I hope it is not too late. I am an ex RCAF war veteran age 74 years and had occasion to be in Kirriemuir on leave in 1945. I attended a banquet on the one night that I stopped over. In addition to being treated very admirably at the dinner and what a dinner it was! – I was asked, along with others, if anyone present was not a member of the Ancient Order of Curlers, and not being a member was promptly given initiation into the Order of Curlers.

It was an occasion I shall never forget, particularly my two guides who were about 6ft 3 or 4 and well built I still remember the ritual as well as the passwords and hand grip. I have always thought that the odds on being in Kirriemuir on the very night of the dinner were one in a million. Well, there it is, gentlemen, or Brethren, I've done it and hope this letter reaches the Order of Curlers and that it is still active. Many thanks once again for that wonderful evening so long ago.

Yours truly

Thomas Kennedy

P.S.

My forehead finally healed from the branding it took – Ha, Ha

See reply on next page

KIRRIEMUIR OBSERVER 24TH FEBRUARY 1866

On Monday our curlers had a stiff match on the Loch of Kinnordy, the cup and the prize stones being played for. Owing to the fresh nature of the day the ice was very heavy, so much so that several had to give in. A good number however, stuck to it and after a severe contest Mr Gilruth, Kilnhill gained the cup with 16 points and Mr Cowpar, Longbank, the stones with a score of 15.

The Reply

1055, Valour Road,
Winnipeg, 4,
Manitoba. R3G 3B9

Malindi,
Brechin Road,
Kirriemuir.
Angus DD8 4BX

14/3/94

Dear Brother Curler Thomas,

Fraternal greetings from Kirriemuir and thanks for your interesting letter which despite there being no 'official' organisation called the 'Ancient Order of Curlers and Forfarshire having disappeared from maps about 50 years ago, our ingenious post office delivered it to the right man. Obviously your brief visit to our wee toon in 1945 was a memorable one as you were initiated into the ancient brotherhood of curlers. More of that later.

I am a member of Kirriemuir Curling Club and despite being 'just' 51 am the longest serving member having joined in 1964. I've been involved with curling management at all levels and for a great many years have been responsible for the organisation of Curlers Courts in and around Kirriemuir. These Courts go back to the earliest days of curling, their original object being to fine curlers for petty demeanours committed on the ice and to initiate new members (or nobodies) into the mysteries of the ancient brotherhood of curlers. K.C.C. hold a court about every two years with a format of fun, frolics and fellowship, probably very similar to your own 'making'.

I had hoped to find mention of your visit in our minutes but unfortunately courts at that time were not recorded and regrettably most of those who had been present have since gone to that large curling rink in the sky. I doubt if you would remember names so long ago but the likes of Jim Annand, Jim Wedderspoon, Sam Pate, Wallace Neilson (still alive) and my late father David McKiddie would certainly have been present. He was the local pharmacist and if you remember having to ----- ---- ---- ---------*, it would have been of his making. Do you recall where or whom you stayed with?

A Canadian connection – every 4 years 22 Canadian Rotary Curlers tour Scotland for 4 weeks, one of the stops being the Kirriemuir area and at Aberdeen they always hold a court for any nobodies in their midst. In the intervening years Scotland sends a team to Ontario/Quebec and I was fortunate to be part of the team in 84. I made many friends there and have returned with my wife and have entertained Canadians back to our home – all though the curling connection.

So – nice to hear from you – glad you did get round to writing and hope this finds you hale and hearty.

Can you remember the responses overleaf?!!!

Yours,

Cameron McKiddie

*Words deleted due to the confidentiality of the Initiation - ED

A transcript of a follow up hand- written letter from Canada

1055 Valour Road
Winnipeg, Manitoba
Canada R3G 3B9

Dear Cameron,

I was very pleased to get a reply to my letter, as I did have my doubts about it. To begin – I have never participated in curling to any extent, just the odd game or so. When I went from England up to Scotland in 1945 I called on my wife's uncle Doddie Scott, who owned a pub in Stirling (you can see I was well connected right from the start!) I told Doddie I was enroute as far north as Aberdeen to see more of the wife's relatives (my relatives were Irish). He asked me when I would be on the road back as he was going to visit his son in law in Kirriemuir and named a certain date. I said I would try and be there (and was).

I think his son in law, also first name Doddie either worked for, or was, the burgh surveyor of Kirriemuir. His wife's first name was Gertie and for the life of me I can't recall young Doddies last name – Smith maybe. I stayed with them along with the wife's uncle Doddie Scott while in Kirriemuir. The evening of the Curling banquet was quite an event & I recall there were 40 ounce bottles on the table about 4 ft apart (long tables) During the course of the evening all those who were not members were asked to stand. I stood up- I honestly can't recall whether anyone else stood up or not. As I told you before I was approached by these two very tall and well built guides to become initiated and wasn't asked one way or another. I was ----- ------* and led up and down steps and turned about and around. I was told to open -- -----* and I was required to 'turn the florin** ----- -- -----* and when - ------ -- --- --- --- -- -- -- -----*. My forehead was then branded with some hot substance, the letters later found to be A.O.C.*** in red. I was then told that I had to cast the rock, and to draw my arm back and then forward in a throwing motion resulting in my arm ----- --- - ----------- -- ---- -----.* Oh Yes. Just prior to O no – I'm wrong here – after turning the florin and throwing the rock – my ---- -----* was removed & it was quite an experience – I was in a darkened room, and there was a large vat with some substance that gave off a bright light & steam or something. Before I could recover from the effect from dark to light, that was when I was branded with the letters A.O.C.

I was then given the pass grip with the ----- ---- --- ----- -- --- -- - ----* and the pass words --- --- ----- .*

I don't recall the names of any other persons at the social that evening. Incidentally just as a matter of trivia, the street I live on, VALOUR ROAD did not always have that name. It was called Pine Street until after World War 1. It seems that three occupants of that street living in the same block in the street, all three were awarded the Victoria Cross for Valour. I think it must be record of some sort. I'm sure there were maybe more than three VC winners from a town or city, but to all be in the same block on the same street is something else.

Well Cameron, I want to thank you for taking the time and trouble to write to me. I don't recall any questions being asked in the ritual, just being given the grip & word.

Yours very sincerely

Tom Kennedy

I love watching curling on T.V. when we have the Brier and the World Cup. That's when you see some fantastic pressure shots.

Tom

What was remarkable was his detailed and accurate account, after a period of 50years
*Words deleted due to the confidentiality of the Initiation Ed.
**Florin – a pre-decimal coin being a 2-shilling piece
*** A.O.C. – Ancient Order of Curlers

18

THE KIRRIEMUIR OBSERVER 19TH JANUARY 1884
Curlers' Dinner

On the evening of Monday last the members of the Kirriemuir Curling Club, to the number of about thirty partook of their annual dinner of beef and greens, purveyed by " mine host" of the Crown Hotel*, (Mr Menzies) in his usual sumptuous manner. T.M.Wilson, Esq., solicitor occupied the chair, and was supported on the right by the secretary of the club, Mr Savage, and on the left by P.G. Duncan, Esq., of Hillhead. The worthy treasurer of the club, Stewart Lindsay. Esq., of Crawford Park discharged the duties of croupier, supported by Messrs Newton, coal-merchant, and Mr Dewar, of the Airlie Arms Hotel. There were also deputations present from two sister curling clubs – Tannadice and Cortachy. After doing ample justice to the good things of this life, the chairman proposed the health of the Queen, and also of the other members of the Royal Family. The croupier then proposed the Army, Navy and Reserve Forces, warmly commenting on the great efficiency of the army, and the indomitable pluck and courage of the navy, together with the enthusiastic ardour, energy, and prowess of the Reserve Forces. He facetiously remarked on the fact that Cortachy had no volunteers; but he repudiated the assertion of a Cortachy man, that if an army appeared near Kirriemuir from the south, Cortachy would soon have plenty of volunteers, - he was sure if an army did appear, the Kirriemuir forces would firmly hold their own. Mr Duncan and Mr Morrison replied. The chairman proposed the Chaplain of the club and Clergy of all denominations, to which Mr Lindsay replied. A curlers' court was then formed, the president acting as "my lord" and Mr John Milne as "my lord officer" – both absolute. Several recalcitrant brethren were repeatedly fined. On the stoup being rouped, it, after keen competition, was knocked down to Mr Newton, coal merchant, who, it is believed, was afterwards offered a handsome profit on the transaction.

On the court being closed, the toast list resumed. The "Town and trade of Kirriemuir," the "Agricultural Interests," and others being duly proposed and responded to. The president of the club. Colonel Grant Kinloch, of Logie, was proposed by Mr Guild, of Herdhill, and was replied to by Mr Wilson, solicitor. The "Kinnordy Trustees" were also proposed and received hearty plaudits for so kindly granting the use of the Forrest Muir curling pond. The chairman, the secretary, the treasurer, and even "his satanic majesty," of the curling club, were all duly honoured, the latter personage being present, replied to the toast of his health amidst roars of laughter. The ladies by Mr Milne was replied to by Mr Lindsay, in terms far too loving and pathetic for pen to portray. Interspersed with song and recitation the evening passed quickly away, and after singing "auld lang syne" the brethren separated, mutually hoping that "John Frost" would give them the opportunity of meeting at an early date.

The Crown Hotel built in 1860 became the well known Ogilvie Arms Hotel around 1898 and in recent years has been converted into flats.

Every Picture Tells a Story – 2

This watercolour painting of the last Grand Match played at Lake of Montieth in 1979 is owned by the editor and also appears on the front cover. At that time Cameron McKiddie was Chairman of Kirriemuir Community Council and council member Fin McKenzie and he were instrumental in setting up the first Art Exhibition of works from local artists. Kirriemuir artist Joyce Grubb submitted a number of paintings including 'The Grand Match'. Joyce's husband Iain had played for the Lindertis Curling Club in that famous match of 1979 and his many photographs of the event were the inspiration for this painting.

On the opening night of the Art Exhibition, Cameron was first in line to purchase the painting.

A poem about the Skip

When the body was first made, all parts wanted to be skip.

The brain insisted that since it controlled everything and did all the thinking that it should skip.

The feet said that since they carry the body up and down the ice they should be the skip.

The hands retorted that since they deliver the stone and mark the card, they should be skip.

The eyes too staked their claim: since they judged the shots and watched the heads, they should be skip.

And so it went on – the heart, the ears and finally the bum!

How all the other parts laughed to think the bum should be skip.

Thus the bum became mad and refused to function.

The brain became feverish, the eyes crossed and ached, the legs got wobbly and the stomach went sick.

All pleaded with the brain to relent and to let the bum be skip.

And so it came to be, that all the other parts did their job, and the bum skipped and played a load of s**t.

Moral: Any bum can be skip.   **Anon**

Kirriemuir Free Press 6th February 1936
FORFAR BONSPIEL CONTROVERSY
Question of Who Has Right To Call It. - RIVAL ORGANISERS.

Forfar Loch has not seen a bonspiel for more than twenty years, but if the frost hardens it seems likely to see two in the space of two days- one tomorrow and one on Sunday. The Angus Curling Province bonspiel is definitely fixed to be held on the Loch tomorrow. This has been officially announced by Mr. David Smith, town clerk of Kirriemuir, who is honorary secretary of the province. But Provost Graham, Forfar, states that he has already received entries, which have been paid for, from 69 rinks for the bonspiel on the Loch — which he has called for Saturday. He points out that the Fothringham Cup and district medals will be played for. When provost Graham called a bonspiel shortly before the last spell of frost broke, Mr. Smith questioned his right to do so, pointing out that the Provost demitted office as secretary in 1933, when he (Mr Smith) was appointed the secretary of the province, which is affiliated to the Royal Caledonian Curling Club. Provost Graham, however, holds that it is his prerogative to call the bonspiel, and meantime a deadlock has been reached. Mr Smith was in Glasgow yesterday, but he left the arrangements in the hands of Mr A.W. Barclay, president of Forfar Curling Club. With the ice on the Loch 4 ½ inches thick generally, and in parts six inches, Mr Barclay called the bonspiel for tomorrow.

The Official One

"The bonspiel called for tomorrow," Mr Barclay explained, "is therefore the official one of the Angus Curling Province. If anyone else chooses to call a bonspiel for Saturday it is unofficial as far as the province is concerned, and entirely on the caller's own responsibility. The province has official permission to hold its bonspiel on Forfar Loch and Mr Smith, or those he appoints, are the only ones who can call the bonspiel on behalf of the province." Mr Barclay added:- "When the bonspiel was run by the now defunct Angus Curling Association, the secretarial work was done by the Provost and his late father, the late Mr D.M.Graham, but he has now no authority whatever to act on behalf of the Angus Province."

Provost Graham, in an interview, said he did not recognise the bonspiel arranged by Mr Smith and Mr Barclay. "The bonspiel I have called for Saturday has been played for many years on Forfar Loch, and is open to all clubs in Angus, West Perthshire and Kincardineshire and is not confined to Angus Province." he said. " I have the trophies and medals in my possession, which will be played for on Saturday." Twenty one degrees of frost were registered at six o'clock yesterday morning and 14 at midday.

Kirriemuir Free Press 13th February 1936
FORFAR CURLING CONTROVERSY
- SPRAYING OF ICE SURFACE LEADS TO COMPLAINTS

The Forfar curling controversy was still in the news over the weekend. A well-intentioned move to improve the ice on Forfar loch did not meet with the approval anticipated. The roughened surface was sprayed with water but the frost was not keen enough to consolidate the surface and curlers complained that it was worse than before. The burgh fire engine was out late on Saturday night spraying part of the ice with water so that when the frost returned a smooth surface would be provided. Unfortunately the frost did not play up, and the part sprayed was water logged and rough on Sunday while skaters ploughed up the soft ice. " No one connected with the Province was consulted." said Mr A.W. Barclay, president of the Forfar Curling Club, on Sunday. "The part affected forms a very large part of the ice it had been intended to use for the Province bonspiel." Councillor Walker, the fire convener, explained that the spraying was done with the best of intentions. The bonspiel, however came off successfully on Tuesday, and all's well that ends well.

Kirriemuir Free Press 20th February 1936

CLEARING UP BONSPIEL MUDDLE.

Custody of trophies problem – CALEDONIAN CLUB TO DECIDE

A further step in the Forfar curling controversy was taken on Monday night, when a meeting of the Province was held in Forfar.

The proceedings were in private, but it is learned that the whole question of the arrangements for future bonspiels and the custody of the trophies has been left in the hands of the Royal Caledonian Curling Club. Another meeting of the Province is to be held at an early date.

Some mystery appears to surround the curling cup presently held by the Alyth Club.

When the Angus Provincial Bonspiel was played on Forfar Loch last Tuesday it was announced that the officials were unable to present it to Catterthun because Alyth, the previous holders, had not brought the trophy with them to the bonspiel, but Catterthun were announced the holders for the ensuing year.

On Thursday at the close of Angus Curling Association Bonspiel on Forfar Loch, the Alyth club were not represented, but, Provost Graham, Forfar, announced that the Fothringham Cup was held by Alyth, from whom it would be secured and forwarded to the winners, namely, the Pitkerro club.

The problem arises – which body has the right to request Alyth to hand over the trophy or trophies? Inquiries made by the "Free Press" indicate that the Alyth club are unlikely to make any move in this direction until they receive official notification from the Royal Caledonian Club.

Future Bonspiels

Ten rinks took part in the Angus Curling Association Bonspiel, arranged by provost Graham. The ice was in perfect order.

It was made clear at a meeting of the Angus Curling Club, held at the interval in the bonspiel, that the association intends to run a bonspiel annually, apart from what the Province may decide to do.

Mr David Ramsay, of Pitkerro, presided, and the secretary and treasurer Provost Graham submitted his report and read the minutes of the previous meeting. The report and balances were approved.

The following office bearers were elected for the ensuing year;

Patron, the Earl of Strathmore; president, Col. Fothringham of Fothringham; vive-presidents, Sir Torqil Munro of Lindertis, and Mr Gavin Ralston, Glamis; secretary and treasurer, Provost Graham; committee representative of Forfar, Evenie Water, Fothringham, Oathlaw, and Glamis.

It was left to the secretary to carry out the arrangements with his committee for the next annual bonspiel.

Independent Body

It was felt at the meeting that the attention of all clubs should be drawn to the fact that the Association is an association comprising all of Angus, East Perthshire, and Kincardineshire.

"It is" said Provost Graham,"an entirely independent body, playing its own bonspiel annually, irrespective of any province or provincial bonspiel which may be played."

At the close of the bonspiel Provost Graham announced that the Fothringham Cup for the rink with the most shots up had been won by the Pitkerro rink, skipped by Mr J. M'Clean, and consisting of A. M'Clean, W.G.Reid, D. Ramsay, and J.M'Clean.

The medal for the club with the highest average up per rink was won by Kirkinch and Nevay, and accepted on behalf of the club by Mr J. Kidd. The presentation of the medal was made by Major Ogilvy.

Kirriemur Free Press 13th February 1936

"ALL IN" ICE HOCKEY ON FORFAR LOCH

KIRRIE LADS THE WINNERS

Kirriemuir lads proved their superiority over their Forfar rivals in ice skating and "all in" ice hockey on Forfar loch on Sunday when a team travelled to Forfar and licked the locals by 14 goals to nil. Teams were not restricted to any specified number, with the result Kirrie were badly outnumbered. But with the redoubtable spirit of their weaver ancestors the Kirrie lads soon had the Forfarians on toast. And, needless to say, the fun was thoroughly enjoyed.

News from New Zealand

In February, 2009 I tried to find the verses omitted from the poem, 'The Old Curler and his Wife' (page 27). Using 'Google' search engine I came across the web page of the Ancient Briton Hotel, New Zealand and after an exchange of e-mails, I obtained further choice material for this book.

The Ancient Briton Hotel is located in Naseby in the South Island. Often referred to as the 'Jewel of Maniototo', Naseby came to prominence in the 1860's with the discovery of gold. The Gold Rush attracted miners from around the world including Scotland and it is said that curling on the frozen lakes was introduced during the severe winters when mining was nigh impossible. 'John Frost' permitting, an annual Bonspiel is held at the nearby village of Oturehua while Naseby itself now boasts an international indoor curling rink.

Ross McMillan who writes under the name 'Blue Jeans' is recognised as one of New Zealand's, finest high country poets. Ross is a member of Otago Central Curling Club and an honorary life member of Naseby Curling Council.

There are almost 40 curling clubs in New Zealand, all but two located on the South Island.

A Curling Song

"Now the winter days are over and the spring is on its way,
And the man who was a curler - he must put his broom away.
Stow away his hat and ribbons, for the door is tightly shut,
On the crampits and the granites in the ancient curling hut.

For we've played the pride of Scotland and the Maple Leaf team too -
We were open to all comers while we wore the Royal Blue,
And we struggled with the Black Hats and the Red Hats and the White,
And we 'played' till 'wee small hours' with the usual curlers' 'skite'.

But you're back now tending cattle, and I'm back now shearing sheep,
In the tiring endless battle with a wife and a brood to keep.
And I wonder somewhat sadly now our ways are far apart,
Will you think, like me, of curling with an aching in your heart.

When the summer sun is burning and the days are filled with heat,
Will you know a sudden yearning for black ice beneath your feet.
Will you hear the old stones roaring as your lonely job you keep,
And the shouting of the curlers and the swishing of the sweep.

With a whiskey for a good shot (and a whiskey for the bad),
And the brothers of the Bonspiel and the good times that we had.
Driving down the Ida Valley with a load of stones and gear,
When the snow was on the mountains and the frost was in the air.

Driving down the Ida Valley when the sun was hardly up,
Where the eager curlers rally for a Silver Curling Cup.
Come the last days of December (though the days are hot as hell),
I know you'll still remember - and I'll drink a toast as well.   **Blue Jeans**

The Old Curler

The old curler stood at the head of the rink.
His broom in one hand - in his other a drink.
He looked at the stone that was nearest 'the pot' -
A black kiwi granite was holding 'the shot'.

He called to his skip "Now you know what to do
It's not one of ours for our colour is blue.
If you 'draw through the port' you will take it away
The Cup will be ours - you've the last stone to play."

He thought of the long days he spent on the ice.
The way his wife spoke - it was not very nice.
Away with the dawn and late home for sup -
All would be redeemed if they brought back the Cup.

Her eyes would light up at the silver so bright,
Her voice would calm down and not go half the night.
(How the cares of a curler's wife weigh like a tonne)
Through a few weeks of winter can she sure carry on.

For a curler drops all at the call of good ice,
His work, pay and home he forgets in a trice,
And a day or a week or a month he could be
Sweeping the stones from 'the hog' to 'the tee'.

He positioned his broom and he asked for 'tee weight'.
"Just draw 'through the port' and we'll sweep you in mate."
But the stone went astray as some stones often do
And a black stone moved up and the Black Hats sat two.

The old curler stood there and gazed at his skip,
His broom and his drink in his woe-begone grip,
"Ask for 'draw port' and you get a 'chap and lie'
It's enough to bring tears to an old curler's eye."

Late that night in the bar, though, his spirits did rise,
The jubilant winners had left with their prize,
But the old curler noticed he wasn't alone
There were plenty more losers there scared to go home.

Blue Jeans

SCOTTISH SPORT IN CENTRAL OTAGO: THE COMPETITIONS AT NASEBY.

(1) A general view of the bonspiel. The rink is formed on smooth, keen ice, the distance between the tees at each end of the rink being forty yards. Brooms are used to clear the ice of snow. (2) Mr. Andy Brown, an old-time player, delivering the stone. (3) Mr. R. S. Black, Mayor of Dunedin, a very keen curling enthusiast. (4) Mr. Tom Lennane (skip), the oldest player at the meeting.

—E. A. Phillips photo.

Curling on Mt. Ida Dam, Naseby, NZ

Women Curling at Naseby, circa 1890

IdaBurn Dam Curling

Extracts from the Annuals of
The Royal Caledonian Curling Club

District Medal Results

> **District Medal awarded by the Royal Caledonian Curling Club to Kirriemuir Curling Club.**
> **Front & back**

Annual 1875

Kirriemuir 33 Balmerino 38   played on 24th December 1874 at Dundee pond, the match taking 3½ hrs.

Annual 1878

Kirriemuir 31 Brechin Castle 34   played on 31st January 1878 at Tannadice, the match taking 3 hours.

Annual 1881-82

Kirriemuir 64 Logiealmond 53   played on 26th January 1881 on Patter Loch, Murthly, the match taking 3h 40m.

Annual 1886-87

Kirriemuir 68 Edzell 48   played on 16th January 1886 on Brechin Castle Pond, the match taking 3h.

Annual 1889-90

Kirriemuir 42 Forfar 66   played on 13th February 1889 on Glamis Pond, the match taking 3h.

> *As an 11-year-old living in Glamis from 1953 I well remember the Curling Pond and while by then there was rarely any curling, it was a favourite place for skating. – Ed.*

Annual 1893

Kirriemuir 43 Forfar 37   played on 29th December 1892 at Forfar, the match taking 3 hours.

Annual Miscellaneous

Annual 1873

Preface begins 'The delay in the publication of the Annual, caused by the Printers' Strike, has been beneficial, in that it has enabled us to publish the Reports of Matches which, in ordinary circumstances, must have stood over till next year.'   *So strikes were a problem then as well -Ed.*

Annual 1875

From a report of a Meeting of the Representative Committee of the RCCC
The Secretary read a letter from the Secretary of the Lintrathen Club, claiming one Rink's expenses to and from Grand Match held at Carsebreck on 24th December 1874, against the Chryston Club, whose rink did not appear. The meeting unanimously, and in terms of the resolution come to at the Annual Meeting of the Club in July 1853 awarded the Lintrathen Club £2, 7s 6d. as modified expenses.

Annual 1878

Many curlers will have seen Dr Foulis Summer Curling Pond, which was exhibited at the Highland and Agricultural Society's Show held in Edinburgh last summer. We understand it has been improved by substituting steel plates instead of wood, as originally laid – which will afford a very good game during the summer, although it is not to be expected that it will ever take the place of curling on ice.

The Old Curler and his wife

(From Chamber's Journal, December 30, 1882)

Quoth the guidman to the guidwife:
'This is the medal day;
Tho' cauld's the wind, the ice is keen,
So I'll gang to the play.'

Quoth the guidwife, wi coaxin' word:
'You winna gang a fit, man.
If you are wise, take my advice,
And by the ingle sit man.'

'I've played before in caulder days,
When glass stood down at zero;
Gi'e me ma crampits and my broom-
I'll play like an auld hero.'

'But ye maun mind that was langsyne,
When you were young and yauld*, man;
But now you're stiff, your blude is thin -
And you have turned auld, man.'

'Wi frost like this, and ice so keen,
Tho' auld, I yet feel young;
Sae bring my bonnet and my plaid
Guidwife, and haud your tongue.'

'A' night you graned wi' rheumaticks,
An' sair, sair, did you wheeze, man;
The cauld would nip your marrow-banes;
Your very blude would freeze, man.'

'You've ruled me lang enough, guidwife;
Henpecked nae mair I'll be;
I'll hae my will – my broom and cramps,
And to the loch I'll go.'

* yauld – energetic * cowe – broom

'What! To the ice, in sic a day?
If you daur cross the floor, man,
I'll hide your cramps, I'll burn the cowe*,
And double-bar the door, man.'

- - - - - - - - - - - - - - - (1)

Each curler looked with ken-set eye,
And played with steady hand;
But surest aye the old man aimed,
The deftest of the band.

He played the draw, he played the guard,
The outwick and the in,
He struck, he raised, he chapp'd & chipp'd,
He wick'd and curled in.
His points ran up; he far outstripped

The curlers young and auld;
He won the Medal – then trudged hame
Through driftin' snaw and cauld.

- (1)

'Ye doited, donner't daft auld carle,
In you I've nae mair faith;
Fling by your plaid – tak' aff your shoon;
This day will be your death.
You now may grane – you now may cough
Like ony croupit wean;
Nae mair blame me, nor this auld house,
But blame the curling stane.

'Atweel, guidwife I played a plisk
When I set aff the day;
But the sun was shinin' clear i' the lift,
An' keen was I to play.
I winna say but what ye're richt,
And that I'm sare to blame;
But see guidwife – haud out your hand –
I've brocht the Medal hame!'

RCCC Annual 1883-4
(1) some verses had been omitted
from the Annual – Ed.

KIRRIEMUIR FREE PRESS 17TH JANUARY 1946
CURLING AND SKATING IN KIRRIEMUIR

The severe frost which has prevailed this week has been much to the liking of curlers and skaters. The pond in the den, especially in the evenings, has been well patronised by skaters of both sexes – especially the youth of the town and district – and with a fine sheet of ice available, they have enjoyed themselves tremendously.

The members of the Kirriemuir Curling Club are also taking full advantage of the hard wintry weather. The curling pond, situated in the vicinity of the Glengate, has just recently been restored to playing conditions, and with the electric lighting again set up over the rinks, games during the day and evenings have already been engaged in by the members. After a slow start, generally speaking, the ice, after a few ends have been played, becomes quite keen, and the devotees of the "roarin' game" are having quite an enjoyable time just now.

'Jock and the Laird'

Jock was the 'ne'er-do-weel'of the district. Bred originally as a mason, he had early taken to devious courses. His first expedition was a moonlight expedition – 'just for the fun of the thing' – involving the capture of a few of Lord Hardup's hares. This episode led to memorable results in Jock's life. The party was surprised and pursued by the keepers, who were aided by the 'polis'; and Jock, having hurt his foot in jumping a dyke, fell prey to the myrmidons of the law. He was smartly fined, and dismissed with the advice not to come back again. Instead of profiting by this admonition, he determined that he would have his money's worth out of the lairds, and that he would not stop poaching till he had imbursed himself by the amount of the fine. Poor Jock found, as many a man has done, both before and since, that it is too easy to begin a coarse of action, but very hard to tell where it may lead or when it may terminate. He gradually drifted away from steady work, and devoted himself more and more to his unlawful pursuits. At last he gave up his mason work entirely, and became one of the numerous class that have no apparent means of livelihood. Old Nannie Trummle, Jock's mother, had many misgivings as to her son's 'ongauns.' Her 'man,' Will Trummle, had been one of the most respectable inhabitants of Rawburn parish.

During his forty years of service as grieve at Windymains,

he had never once had a 'thrawn word wi' the master.' He and Nannie had wished their only child to follow in his father's footsteps, and for a time Jock drove 'the orra horse' at Windymains. Tiring, however, of 'the horse' and also perhaps of parental oversight, he went off without consulting any one and got bound as an apprentice to old Sandy Bathgate, the builder.

It was while working with him that he fell in with the wild blades who tempted him to join their nocturnal adventures, with the result which we already know. At the time of our story he was known as the most successful and daring poacher in the country-side. Time after time he had been fined with the ever-increasing severity. He had repeated got 'saxty days' for assaults on gamekeepers, and several broken ribs gave evidence of the roughness with which these exasperated individuals had treated him. In fact there was an understanding among them that it was no good getting a case against Jock Trummie, and that a sound thrashing was the best thing to give him. To do Jock justice, he did not often give them the chance.

Most men, however bad have some redeeming points in their character. Jock had at least two. One of these was his affection for his old mother, and the other was the fact that he was a keen curler. We may perhaps count as a third that Jock had managed to win the heart of bonny Jean M'Alpine, the daughter of Lord Hardup's head-keeper. Strange though it may appear, it was a well-known fact that 'the keeper's dochter has ta'en up wi' poacher Jock. ' They had forgathered on one occasion at Windymains 'kirn,' and Jock, while conveying her home through the moonlit woods of Castle Hooly, had deepened the impression made on Jean's soft heart during the evening, and had won her promise to be his 'lass.' Here was poaching with vengeance! In vain her father stormed, and threatened to string him up among the weasels and 'hoodies' behind the kennels if he dared to venture near the door. It is well known that 'love laughs at locksmiths,' and I am afraid irascible fathers are equally derided by the blind boy. Reason or none, Jean determined to stick to her poacher 'lad' and the devoted pair found means of meeting at intervals. While loving Jock with all her heart, Jean naturally disliked his mode of life exceedingly. 'Oh, Jock,' she would say, looking up pleadingly into his face, 'wull ye no' gie up that terrible poachin'? I'm feared ye get yersel' shot, or tak' the life o' some o' the keepers, ye're sic a regairdless chap.' 'Weel Jean, my lass,' Jock had on one occasion replied, 'I'm no' sae bad as yer father thinks. If I could get a chance o' a steady job I wad tak' it; but, eh, wuman! Wha wud gie "poacher Jock" onything to dae? As for bein' regairdless, I'll promise ye no' to risk onything.' Since that time Jock had made various fruitless attempts to settle down to steady work, but his reputation was very much against him. 'Give a dog a bad name and you may as well hang him,' proved to be a true saying in his case.

He had recently been casting wistful glances at a situation which happened to be vacant, and which would have suited him down to the ground. This was the post of underkeeper to Mr Hope Smith of Netherwood, usually known in the parish as 'the Laird.'

Jock knew full well that any application of his would be treated with scorn, but all the same he could not help thinking how well he was suited for the work, and how cosy he and Jean might be in the snug cottage up at Burnbrae.

Now let us see how the wheel of fortune sometimes brings to pass most unlikely events. Jock, as we have seen, was a keen curler. No better ever soled a stone. It was said that he had once walked forty miles to take part in a match, and had pulled it out of the fire by his splendid play at the last end. The season in which the following occurrences took place was an uncommonly severe one, so that devotees of the roaring game had their full swing. In fact, some of their less enthusiastic neighbours were beginning to say, 'Are ye no' tired o' the curlin' yet?' in a tone which implied that these misguided curlers were keeping up the frost for their own benefit. There had been several severe tussles between Rawburn and other clubs, in which, for the most part, the Rawburn men had been victors. There remained one club to play, and that the strongest in the district, hailing from Treddleton, the market-town. A match was arranged on Rawburn ice, the day was fixed, and the only thing that was left was to get up as strong rinks as possible for the occasion. This, as it turned out was no easy matter; for, while Riddell of Howfaugh and the minister had their rinks full, the Laird was in terrible difficulties. Stoddart the mason, his third player, was down with an attack of influenza, and Jamie Dudgeon, the late underkeeper, had removed to a distance. The Laird could easily have got men to play with him, but not the kind that he wished.

In his extremity it was suggested to him that Jock Trummle might be available. 'What! That poaching fellow!' he exclaimed. 'Would he dare to come on the ice if I am there?' 'Deed, Laird,' was the reply, 'Jock's no' easy frichtet, an' ye maun mind that on the ice the best curler is the best man. If ye had Jock for third

hand, we could easy fit ye wi' a second, an' then ye would gie they Treddleton bodies their wark to lick ye or I'm cheatet.' Though it went sorely against the grain, the Laird was at last convinced that this was the only feasible arrangement, and a plenipotentiary was despatched to treat with Jock.

'Weel,' said that worthy, after cogitating for some time, I'll no deny that I'm fell keen o' a gemm, an' if the Laird'll no' be ower sair on me for yon plaisants, I'll play for him.' Being assured that Mr. Hope Smith had undertaken that bygones should be strictly considered as things of the past, Jock closed the bargain.

See him, then, arriving at the Rawburn pond on the appointed day, 'the cynosure of neighbouring eyes.' Across his shoulders he bears his father's old plaid, each end of which contains one of Jock's favourite curling-stones, fashioned by his own hands from a boulder found on Windymains farm. These stones had figured in many a match, and were known as 'the Craigies,' from the fact that their native boulder lay originally on the banks of the Craighope burn. Under his arm Jock carries a freshly cut broom 'kowe,' which he playfully whisks round the ears of the urchins who shout as he passes, 'Jock there's the Bobby!'

''Morning, Jock,' said the Laird, who was determined to be as gracious as possible to his old enemy; I hope you are in good form today, as we are expecting great things from you.' 'I'll dae my best, Laird,' replied Jock, 'ye may lippen upo' that; an' if I'm no oot o' my ord'nar, I can aye manage to shute gey straucht.' This was said with such an innocent look that the Laird thought best to give no heed to its doubtful meaning, but contented himself with asking his men to come and try their stones before the match began.

We shall not weary the patience of our readers by describing at length this famous game, which is still spoken of in the parish as 'Jock Trummle's match.' Suffice it is to say that it was a very close thing all through. At intervals during the progress of the game Jock's voice might be heard above the general din adjuring his fellow players to ' gie the Laird legs!' or ejaculating, 'Man, Laird, gin ye hit that yin, I'll gie ye an orange!' or, 'D'ye see that stane? Gie that yin saxty days!'

When the stipulated number of ends had been played

on two of the rinks, it was found that Riddell had tied with his opponents, while the minister was three down. The Laird at this juncture was finishing his second last end, and stood one up. It looked, however, as if Treddleton would score. Their leading stones lay close to the tee and were well guarded. Jock Trummle had spent one of his stones in a vain attempt to break off the guards, and the Laird was directing him as to the second. He saw that an inwick from an outlying stone would take the shot, but this stone was half- guarded and lay wide from the tee. 'Jock,' he called ' do you see the inside of that stone?' 'Ay,' responded Jock; 'but can I wan at it?' ' Yes, if you run the guard close, and take the in-cheek. Now come away with some running and elbow in, and if you take the shot I'll give you – anything you ask!' ' Dune wi' you, Laird!' shouted Jock, a brilliant idea flashing through his mind.

He walked up the rink, and took a look at the lie of the stones, muttering to himself, 'A gey kittle shot. I hae ta'en waur, but there's an awfu' heap dependin' on this yin.' Having carefully looked to the sole of his stone, Jock took deliberate aim, and sent it birling up the ice, amid cries of 'Weel pitten doon, whatever it dis!'

With breathless expectation the onlookers watched its progress. It seemed as if it must touch the guard; but no, past it glided, took the in-wick beautifully, and running right for the winner, drove it off the tee and lay in its place. The air was rent with shouts of exultation on the part of the Rawburn men, while their opponents shook their heads and were fain to admit, 'A gey bonny shot yon.' ' You, for a curler, Jock!' shouted the Laird in an ecstasy of joy, 'Give me a shake of your hand,' and he nearly wrung Jock's hand off as they met in the middle of the rink. 'Ay, ye auld Craigies,' said Jock, as he fondly flicked the successful stone with his broom, 'ye'll maybe dae yer maister a gude turn yet.'

The Treddleton skip in vain tried to drive up some of the guards on the winner. 'Lock that door Laird,' was Jock's command, as he brought the Laird up to a weak spot in the defence. No change was made by the other stones, and the Laird finished the end two up. There remained one end to play, and in order to win the match Rawburn must score at least two. This they managed to do with ease, beating their opponents by three shots and pulling off the match by a majority of two. Before leaving the ice the Laird came up to Jock and said: 'Now I must redeem my promise.

Tell me what I can do for you. I consider that you won the match for us, and you richly deserve a reward.' Jock took off his cap, scratched his head, and, after a little hesitation, said: 'Faith ! Laird, I need nae reward for playin' on the ice. Hooever, sin' you've said it, there's juist yae thing that I wud like to ask ye for, an' that's Jamie Dudgeon's place.' 'Nonsense!' said the Laird, completely taken aback by such an audacious request, 'that is utterly impossible.'

'Impossible, Is't?' responded Jock, 'I thocht it might be possible that a gentleman wud keep his word, even though it was only wi' a poacher.' 'Yes, yes, but of course when I made that promise I was a little excited, and I did not think of your taking me up in this way.' 'Aweel,' said Jock resignedly, 'ye can gang back on your word gin you like. I'll ask ye for naething else,' and with this he turned abruptly away. 'Stop, stop!' exclaimed the other, 'we can't part in this way. What I mean is that it would never do to put you, a notorious poacher, in a position of trust, where you would be constantly tempted to defraud your employer.' 'Eh, Laird,' replied Jock, 'ye ken little of human natur'. Man! there wud be nae temptation to tak' what ye could get sae easy. D'ye no see that it's the danger an' pride o' gettin' the better o' the keepers that gies poachin' its main attraction? Noo.' continued he earnestly, 'gie me a chance. I swear to ye ye'll never regret it. I'll be a faihfu' servant. Few ken mair than I dae aboot thae wild craturs, an' I gie ye my solemn word that ne'er a yin wull gang the wrang gait for me.' 'But,' argued the Laird, still unwilling to be convinced, 'what about your former companions? Would they be constantly trying to get at you, and inducing you to make away with the game?' 'Na, na, Laird, I hae nae companions. I had eneuch o' that at the first ploy that started me on that road. A'that I hae dune, I hae dune mysel', an' there's no' a man that can say he was ever oot at nicht wi' me sin syne.' 'But, Jock,' asked the Laird, 'is it not a fact that you are rather fond of drink?' 'Drink!' said Jock, scornfully, 'I never cared for drink. I never was fou a' my life. I may tak' an antrim dram noos and thans, but never mair. An' let me tell ye, Laird, a man that can say that efter the life that I've lived wud no be muckle tempted to tak' it when he had a steady job.' 'Well, well, come up to the House tomorrow morning at half-past ten, and we will have a talk over it. But remember,

I do not consider that my promise binds me to consent to any such arrangement as you have proposed.'

Jock went away over the hills to his mother's that night with a light heart. The curlers would not hear of him removing his stones, so he stowed them away in the curling-house, saying in an undertone, as he tenderly handled them, 'Ye dour auld beggars! Ye are Jock's best friends yet.' Next morning he turned up punctually at Netherwood House, and after a long confab with the Laird – the latter part of which Stobbs, the head-keeper, was admitted – gained his point, and was engaged as under-keeper.

This was the turning-point in Jock's life. It seemed to make a new man of him. His first proceeding was to march up to Mr M'Alpine's house, and, before that gentleman could find breath to protest against such presumption, demand his daughter in marriage. Explanations having ensued, it was found that John Turnbull, under-keeper to Mr. Hope Smith, was a very different individual from 'poacher Jock,' and the whilom incensed parent was induced to give a dignified assent.

Many happy days did Jock and his bonny Jean spend at Burnbrae. He became as diligent and successful in his work as he had formerly been at his unlawful occupation; and, eventually, on the death of the worthy Stobbs was promoted to his situation. Often did he and his master, when tramping home together after a long day on the heather or among the turnips, recall the curling match that made a man of 'poacher Jock' and secured to the Laird a trusty and life-long friend.

R.C.C.C. Annual 1896-97

Minutes that Mattered

Quoted verbatim from the Minute Books of Kirriemuir Curling Club

While of primary interest to members of Kirriemuir Curling Club, the minutes, which appear, do give a brief history of significant events in the development of the club. One recurring vein is procuring a site for a new pond; financing it, only for a few years later to receive complaints of its dilapidated state and another search for a new pond.

1st November 1872

It was moved by Mr. Shepherd and unanimously agreed that a vote of thanks be accorded to Mr. Grant for his services as secretary during the last 16 years.

The secretary laid before the meeting a circular from Andrew Lowson, President of the Arbroath and St Vigeans Curling Club proposing that this club should join in a scheme for forming an artificial pond near Guthrie Station for the purpose of supplying a want felt by many players in Forfarshire. Mr. Grant moved that this club should take no action meantime for carrying out this proposal.

24th October 1873

Annual subs increased from 2/6 to 3/6 *(12½p – 17½p)*

The meeting resolved that the pond be lengthened by 9 feet and that a new arrangement for supplying the pond with water be carried out in accordance with the plans furnished by Mr. Fairweather of Newport and that the expense thereof be allocated equally to the several members of the club after the same has been ascertained and that the secretary be authorised to apply to Contractors for estimates for the work to be submitted to the Committee of management for their consideration and decision.

6th July 1878

The meeting having been called by convenor Mr. Farquharson to consider the propriety of erecting a new Curling House – the Committee carefully inspected the present erection and as it is in a very dilapidated state, they unanimously recommended that a new structure should at once be erected, - such structure to be composed of brick and to be erected towards the centre of the South side of the Pond with suitable steps to it from the ice.

26th September 1881

On the motion of Mr. Guild it was unanimously agreed that the annual subscription shall be five shillings each instead of three shillings & six pence as formerly until debts of the new curling house be cleared off.

11th October 1889

The Secretary was instructed to write Mr. Lyell of Kinnordy to endeavour to arrange with him to receive a deputation from the club with the object of securing a piece of ground near the town suitable for a curling pond.

Chief Magistrate Wilson Cup 1889

The Secretary informed the meeting that Chief Magistrate Wilson had intimated his desire to present to the Club for Annual competition a silver jug or cup or medal whichever the Committee agreed on, of the value of not less than £3. 3s The meeting cordially and heartily thanked the Chief magistrate for this gift – another tangible proof of the friendly interest he has always taken in the welfare of the club.

Cup Detail

1st October 1890

Chief Magistrate Wilson was awarded a hearty vote of thanks for the very handsome silver cup he had presented to the club for Annual Competition.

10th October 1892

Committee appointed to meet Mr. Lyell of Kinnordy to endeavour to acquire ground from him for the purpose of making a new pond.

6th October 1893

A Committee was appointed to meet Mr. Lyell of Kinnordy and endeavour to acquire ground from him for a new pond. *Things moving slowly? – Ed*

28th September 1894	A committee were appointed to meet Sir Leonard Lyell Bart M.P. of Kinnordy & endeavour to acquire ground from him. *5 years of endeavour without result? – Ed*
5th September 1902	With reference to the continuous efforts of the club to get a suitable piece of ice Messrs Martin & Dewar explained to the Meeting that they had met with Sir Leonard Lyell Bart of Kinnordy who had graciously given his consent to allow the Club to play upon the Loch of Kinnordy and also allow the Club to erect a Curling House there. *OK, it's only taken 10 years*
24th October 1902	The Committee reported having met Sir Leonard Lyell at the proposed site and along with him staked off the ground required for the erection of new Curling House. Plans with relative specifications of new house were submitted, & after discussion it was agreed to accept the offer of Mr. Charles Ogilvy to erect a new house at a sum not exceeding £50.
11th October 1911	The question of obtaining a new pond was discussed at length & the Secretary was instructed to call a public meeting of the Town's People for Friday 27th within the Small Public Hall. *Approx. 8 years & looking for a new site!*
4th October 1912	The Secretary reported as to the negotiations which had taken place regarding a new Pond, and it was remitted to the Committee to inspect the Ground on the Logie Estate adjoining the Southmuir and report thereanent.
30th October 1912	The Secretary reported to the Meeting the negotiations which had taken place in regard to the acquisition of ground for a new Pond, and in connection therewith there was submitted to the Meeting a Plan of a piece of ground at North Mains of Logie. Mr. Carnegie reported that General Kinloch was agreeable to give the ground on terms to be arranged with the Tenant, Mr. Milne. Mr. Milne who was present, signified his willingness to give the ground at the average rent per acre for his farm. Mr. Carnegie reported that Mr. Bruce, Burgh Surveyor, had taken levels of the ground and estimated the cost of the formation of the Pond to be about £60.
25th November 1912	The secretary reported the negotiation between the factor for General Kinloch and the Committee of the Club regarding the removal of the old house used as a Pig Sty at the North West corner of the ground and it was arranged to pay General Kinloch Five Pounds on condition that the North Boundary of the Curling Pond should be the South face of the said house, and that the Tenant of the farm should be entitled to remove same at his convenience but the Curling club would be entitled to such stones therefrom as they require. It was also understood that the Curling Club should have the privilege of access by cart or trap when necessary from the Public Road along the South boundary of the burn to the Pond. 
9th October 1913	The arrangements for the opening of the new Pond were taken into consideration, when it was resolved that Glamis, Lintrathen, Cortachy and Lindertis Clubs be asked to send one Rink each –
18th October 1921	Reverend William Addison appointed Chaplain to the club. *who would retain this position until 1928 - Minister of the Barony Church, Kirriemuir & uncle to the Editor*
10th October 1930	D. McKiddie elected to Entertainment Committee. The subscription was raised to 5/6.

26ᵗʰ October 1930	A meeting of the committee was held at 16, Bank Street *(David McKiddie's Pharmacy and ultimately the Editor's Optical Practice)* on 26ᵗʰ Oct., Vice President M.B. Wallace in the chair. The business of the meeting was to receive a report from the sub committee re artificial ice rink. The Interim Secy. read a letter from the Burgh Surveyor of Carnoustie, giving details of a rink laid in concrete, the cost of which was £200. Report of possible sites for a rink for the K.C.C. was submitted and two sites were selected as likely. One situated in the Den the other at the rear of Lochmill Cottages in a field at present rented by Jas. Kidd.
3ʳᵈ November 1931	It was agreed to open the new rinks with a match President v Vice President on the first available ice after Monday Nov. 9ᵗʰ.
7ᵗʰ February 1933	The secretary intimated he had received 48 entries for the Redhurst Cup, which was presented for play by Mr. Chas Ogilvy. It was decided to play for this Cup by rinks.
14ᵗʰ October 1936	The secretary was instructed to purchase one dozen pairs of galoshes to be hired out at 3d per game.
18ᵗʰ October 1937	It was carried that the office of President to be held for two years only. Mr. J. Lindsay agreed to show a blue light in his window at High Street when there was ice at the Glengate rinks.
16ᵗʰ October 1945	The Joint Secy. Mr. Jas Wedderspoon then reported on the condition of the rink. He estimated that round £3 would be required to put it in playing condition.
30ᵗʰ September 1946	It was agreed to enter all the competitions at the Dundee Ice Rink.
19ᵗʰ September 1947	It was the feeling of the meeting that in view of the withdrawal of basic petrol in November it would be advisable to try for as much ice as possible in the early part of the year.
28ᵗʰ April 1950	The following Office Bearers were elected.
	President – D.McKiddie *Father to Editor*
20ᵗʰ April 1965	The meeting agreed that it would be in the best interests of the Club to explore the possibility of the disposal of the rinks in the Glengate & thus save some expense as eventually no use was made of these facilities.
30ᵗʰ May 1974	C. McKiddie elected President.
	In the absence of Ian Ewart on holiday the Secretary intimated that Mr. Ewart & Mr. Warden (Fothringham) had expressed a wish to provide a trophy for annual competition between the clubs. The game would be played on a 3-rink basis.
14ᵗʰ May 1975	It was agreed that in view of the increasing petrol costs each passenger will pay the driver 25p towards defraying his expenses.
16ᵗʰ August 1978	Mr McKiddie asked if anyone would be interested in a curling weekend at Green Hotel, Kinross. Various members expressed interest and Mr. McKiddie undertook to make the necessary enquiries and arrangements.
25ᵗʰ April 1979	C. McKiddie appointed Secretary.
	Points Cup – 4 rinks – additional handicap section – cup to be presented by C. McKiddie.
	Pairs Competition – 18 teams of 2 – 5 ends only i.e. 2 games per rink Final –10 ends. Teams drawn. Trophy to be presented by Neil Elder.
	Bonspiel – 8 teams of 4. Skips drawn and play lead. Cup to be presented by Stan Milne. *3 new competitions & trophies presented in one year*
23ʳᵈ April 1980	The Secretary reported that the Ed Weighton Trophy had been presented to Kirrie Club by Mrs Weighton for annual competition with Aberlemno Club.
29ᵗʰ April 1981	A new Junior League Competition of 5 teams restricted to non-skips would be introduced if 8 sheets of extra ice could be obtained.
28ᵗʰ April 1982	Jim Strathearn appointed Ice master at the Glengate Rink with the earnest hope that every endeavour be made to have the rink ready. *Reconditioning outdoor rinks*

27th April 1983	President John Gilmour thanked the Secy. for his continuing good work and mentioned the great fellowship enjoyed in the new annual match against Panmure.
25th April 1984	Iain Grubb presented to the club a handsome Cup from the now disbanded Bonnie Cord Curling Club. This cup would in future be called the Bonnie Cord Cup and be presented to winners of the Spring League. *Previously known as the Junior League*
	Jim Strathearn reported that the rink had been prepared for use but lack of suitable frost meant no play last season.
20th April 1988	Mike McVittie complained of no soup on menu for AGM meal. *Soop, soop!*
19th April 1989	It was proposed that Redhurst teams be increased to eight and discussion followed until Dave Torrie *(the only sober one?)* pointed out there were 9 teams currently. It was agreed to increase to 10 teams.
13th April 1994	The Secretary said that Brown Construction had stated their requirement of the site of the old curling pond in the Glengate. A legal document had been studied by several members of KCC & it was apparent that in view of the dereliction & disrepair of the old rink, the piece of land had reversed (under the terms of the agreement) to the original owners or their subjects – now Brown Construction, without payment. The Sec. was instructed to write to Brown Cons. to say that KCC would comply with the terms, but in the circumstances, perhaps a donation to the Club as a gesture of goodwill might be in order. *High hopes did not materialise*
8th April 1998	The President acknowledged the excellent inter club success Kirrie had achieved mentioning in particular Cameron McKiddie's rink winning the Area 9 Bonspiel, Mike McVittie's winning the Callander Trophy and Alistair Melrose winning the Forfar Points. Russell Hamilton's success in achieving 3rd place in the Wilson League was also mentioned.
9th April 1997	After discussion it was agreed that, with the Bicentenary in mind, subs. be increased gradually, & that extra funds generated be placed in a separate account.
11th April 2001	David Lang, having won the club points competition went on to win the Forfar Points by a record margin.

Kirriemuir Free Press 19th January 1956

CURLERS BONSPIEL ABANDONED – Tradition Was Upheld

It is said that when the Strathmore curlers hold a bonspiel there is sure to be a thaw. This was certainly proved on Monday when one hundred and sixty curlers from nineteen clubs had to leave Stormonth Loch, near Blairgowrie. The Strathmore Province Bonspiel was abandoned owing to water on the ice.

In the early morning conditions were perfect, but soon after play began a thawing wind blew from the south-west. As more and more water gathered on the ice some of the curlers had difficulty in sending their stones the length of the "head." Perfect conditions have not prevailed for some time, the last bonspiel having taken place in December 1952.

Kirriemuir Free Press 12th November 1959

KIRRIE CURLERS MAKE HISTORY
– DECISIVE PROVINCE BONSPIEL TRIUMPH

Kirriemuir Curling Club made history at Dundee when for the first time in the club's long existence, they succeeded in winning the Angus Province Bonspiel, and by virtue of that triumph, annexed the Rescobie Trophy. The rink comprising Alan Clark, W. Christie, J.A. Franchis and Eric Brown (skip) defeated Pearsie skipped by Chas. Craik, by 21 shots to 4, while the other Kirrie ink composed of Rev. F.G. McLaren, M. Brown, G.P. Grant and David McKiddie (skip) beat Lindertis 17 shots to 10. the overall victory gave Kirrie curlers a 24 shot margin. Eric Brown by being skip of the highest up rink, won the Royal Caledonian Curling Club medal, while along with himself, the other members of his rink, won pewter tankards.

Kirriemuir Free Press 22nd January 1959

CURLERS "WAR" WITH WEATHER
Return Of Jack Frost

On lochs, ponds, and asphalt rinks throughout Scotland recently, curlers have been revelling in the traditional outdoor atmosphere ----white hillsides under a red sun, black stones on black ice. In recent years, outdoor curlers have had a thin time of it. The 1959 freeze-up, the hardest since the war, is therefore all the more welcome.

Scottish curlers have fought a bitter war with the weather down the ages. Before the big indoor rinks set the ancient game on a sure foundation, ensuring seven months of continuous play each year, old time curlers, the helpless victims of Jack Frost, spent their winters anxiously watching thermometers.

The old curling books are full of stories of plans for parish bonspiels, plans which went aft agley as sudden thaws shattered all hopes. For years on end, they waited with scarcely a game to keep the spirits up. Apparently, the many disappointments only made them more eager to take advantage of any ice that came along. And, of course the weather relented occasionally. The winter of 1846 inspired the following song—

> *Johnny Frost is back again,*
> *The queer auld body's back again,*
> *Tell the news to curling men*
> *Johnny Frost is back again:*
> *Johnny thocht he was to blame*
> *For staying a' last year at hame,*
> *Quo' he I'll just draw on my breeks*
> *An gie them twa, three Curling weeks.*

Living near to nature, at the beck and call of the frosts, curlers evolved recognition signals as they prepared for the curling season. Some used to hang out wet handkerchiefs outside their windows, returning now and then to check by the stiffening whether the night was freezing or not. Rev. James Taylor, who wrote a curling book in 1884, reported that favourable symptoms were a ringing earth and a ringing air, and a whole lot of stars without a cloud in the sky.

Today most curlers in Scotland enjoy their favourite game irrespective of weather conditions. Nine indoor rinks serve the community from Aberdeen to Ayr. But the outdoor game continues to delight and invigorate, and curlers are eagerly awaiting the go-ahead for the year's highlight – the Grand Match between the North and South of Scotland at Loch Leven. The latest report is that a slight thaw has melted the snow covering and caused rutted ice, but there is still a definite hope that the big game will go on – on the safety minimum of 5½ inches of ice.

Kirriemuir Free Press 29th January 1959
Local Curlers at Loch Leven

The Grand Curling Match, which took place for the first time since 1935 at Loch Leven last Tuesday was won by the South, who scored 1354 shots to the north's 1335. Over 1000 curlers took part, and the scene on the loch was impressive. There was about 2000 spectators.

A rink from Kirriemuir was present, and with the original opponents from Glasgow failing to turn up, they played against a rink from Brought ferry. After a keenly contested game, the Kirrie curlers emerged winners by 14 shots to 12. The rink comprised L. Guthrie, J. Fearn, Wm. Irvine and B.G. Carnegie (skip)

The Curler Of Last Resort

When ever you think
That you can't find a rink
And the match you will have to abort.
Let me enter a plea,
Ye can aye send for me
I'm the curler of last resort.

If you're short of a lead
I'm the man that you need.
Though the odd stone could be a bit short.
Or fly through the house
As quick as a mouse
I'm the curler of last resort.

I can shift every stone
But especially our own.
That looks to be scoring the shot.
My best chap and lie
Wishes our stones bye-bye
I'm the curler of last resort.

If you ask for a guard I will play it too hard.
For "shot" to me sounds like "short"
If the rink you would clear
The hog I won't near
I'm the curler of last resort.

But keep mind of the day
When you started to play
And your game was a different sort
It was not me but you
Who hadn't a clue.
You were curler of last resort.

I threw out my kipper
And pulled on a slipper
To try to improve at the sport.
But it turned out a farce
When I fell on the ice
I'm still curler of last resort.

Originally from
Stonehouse in
Lanarkshire, Paddy
picked up his name
and lilt from many
years working in
Ireland.
A late entry into the
curling fraternity, he
had but a few years
with Kirrie Curling
Club before dying
from cancer.
His many poems
show him as a man
of humour,
compassion and
courage including
this one-

Big C?
No me!
Whit'll A dae?
Go tae Reekie
Linn
And jump in?
No way!
No' me!

Paddy Liddle

The Science of Curling

There's men in this nation
Need no explanation
Concerning Newton's' Laws of Motion
Those to whom I refer,
In case you should err
Are those of the curling devotion.

By obeying these laws
You can curl without pause
And beat every rink in the nation.
This simple device
Overrules any ice
And puts rival skips in their station.

*Everybody continues in a state of rest or uniform motion in a straight
line until it is acted upon by an external force.*

Newton's; first law
Is nae bother at a'
Be ye second, third, skip or the lead.
All you have to do
Is play the stone true
With proper direction and speed.

*The rate of change of momentum of a body is proportional to the applied
force and acts in the same direction.*

The harder you throw
The faster you go
As you set the stone out on its trip
If you have a good eye
It will land bye and bye
Just where you were told by the skip.

*For every force or action there is an equal force or reaction
which acts in the opposite direction.*

But the force of your thrust
You have power to adjust
By increasing the force of reaction
Gie the stane a guid burl
To increase its curl
So increasing the ice's attraction.

Whenever you try
A good chap and lie
It's a sample of Newton's law 3.
For the lie stops the stone
And goes off on its own
The physics is easy to see.

If momentum you keep
You can forcefully sweep
Reducing the reacting drag
Just obey Newton's laws
And without other cause
You'll soon have the game in the bag.

Paddy Liddle KCC

38

AREA 9 - ROYAL CALEDONIAN
CURLING CLUB

Cameron McKiddie,
Area 9 Secy/Treas.,
16, Bank St.,
Kirriemuir
Ph (01575) 72777 or 72086

23 rd March, 1988

The Secretary
Royal Caledonian
Curling Club,
2, Coates Crescent,
Edinburgh.

Dear Sir,

Following my phone call earlier this month it was determined that bank credits from D.T. Curling Verland E.V. for £50 and from Nederlandse Curling Bond for £14 had been remitted in error to the account of Area 9 R.C.C.C. I therefore enclose a cheque for £64 together with copy Advice Notes.

My action in revealing this fruitful source of revenue of which the above is just the tip of the ice-berg has understandably not endeared me to the management Committee of Area 9 R.C.C.C. as this will seriously jeopardise our future budget.

While our annual management Committee party, funded entirely by the generosity of our curling brotherhood overseas, will still go ahead at Gleneagles on the first Friday of April 1988, a more modest venue will be required in the future.

While we cannot, at this late date, cancel the four 350 SL's prizes for the winning rink of our Area 9 Knockout competition this year, next year's winners will have to be content with a more modest Montego each.

Salaries to our Area Representatives who have tended to hog most of it, as they do on and off the ice will have to be reduced to four figures.

Advanced plans to permanently freeze Forfar loch to provide a Grand Match every year no longer look financially viable.

It will come as no surprise to you that in view of this upheaval that I have been forced to tender my resignation as of the 7th April 1988.

Yours in Curling,

Cameron McKiddie

Cameron McKiddie.

Enc.

THE RCCC REPLY

The Royal Caledonian Curling Club

2 COATES CRESCENT, EDINBURGH EH3 7AN
Telephone 031-225 7083

1st April 1988

Mr C. McKiddie
Area 9 Secy/Treas.
16, Bank St
Kirriemuir

Dear Mr McKiddie,

Thank you for your letter of 23rd March with enclosed cheque. We are glad you took the precaution of forwarding this by Securicor.

As I write this letter today I am tempted to deliver it personally to your party at Gleneagles, but unfortunately, my own transport provided by the R.C.C.C., is at the farriers being re-shod.

I presume that following your resignation on 7th April you will be enjoying your retirement in some tax-haven and look forward to receiving a postcard.

Yours sincerely,

A.C.B. Guild

Kirriemuir Herald
23rd November 1961
Curling Club Annual Dinner

>>> many visitors from neighbouring clubs were present and the toast to them was given by J.R.Arnott and replied to by T. Hay(Panmure). Both gave highly entertaining speeches, and in delving into the archives of his own club, Mr. Hay found out that almost 100 years ago a challenge had been issued by his club to the Kirrie club and accepted by them. This had been revived and the outcome would be reported at a later date.

Kirriemuir Herald
12th January 1967

One would have thought that this game would be sufficient for the one day, but Bill Lees, Ian Ewart and Jim Moffat immediately took to the ice again to compete in the final of the Redhurst Cup. This fixture had been brought forward to enable Sandy Hardie to make a last attempt at capturing the trophy before his departure to Canada. It would be nice to relate that Sandy finally succeeded, but Bill Lee's rink of Willie Mills, Jim Moffat and C.Cattanach proved too good on this occasion and Sandy, despite being shown the miniature cup he could take as a permanent souvenir of happy days with Kirrie Curling Club went under 15-8.

The editor newly married on 7th January purchased Sandy's house & still lives there today

The Roaring Game
Reprinted from the Globe, January 13, 1893

England, which has 'caught on' so tenaciously to the Scottish game of golf, might do worse than follow it up with the Scottish pastime of curling. Like golf, it is a recreation which is suitable for old and young; it does not call for violent exertion on the part of the player, nor yet is it beneath the consideration of the agile and athletic. All it demands are a certain degree of enthusiasm, a pair of Ailsa Craig or Aberdeen granite projectiles, a broom, a sheet of ice and no dislike to alcohol. Some people have been known to play without the alcoholic accompaniment, but they have never been trusted to represent a province at a bonspiel.

>>>>>>>>>>>>>>>>>>>>*

Golfing in the North, like deer-stalking and salmon fishing, is a game for the gentles (sic), but in curling is the germ of that social equality which we shall enjoy when we reach Henry Georgeism – or the grave. In the hollow behind the hamlet, where the larches stand starkly out against a white world, and the black, well-swept ice-rink trolls a merry monotone,

liberty, equality, and fraternity have as much meaning as they ever can have in an imperfect world, for the factor plays with the tenant; and the blacksmith, who has poached proclivities, is simply 'Sandy, my chiel' to the landlord with whose coverts he is said to be nocturnally too familiar. >>* Even the clergy are not too strictly denominational on these occasions, and the Established and Free Kirk clergymen forget their old ecclesiastical differences in the new rivalry of the rink. But the United Presbyterian minister is rarely a curler, for the United Presbyterians are antagonistic to the liquor traffic with which the game is, in popular mind, inseparably associated.

The old notion, so prevalent in England, that the Scots puts business and the getting of money before all other earthly interests, gets a severe shock when the wind is north and the ice 'hauds.' It takes a terrible amount of self-denial to keep a curler off the ice on a Sunday, but nothing short of his own burial can keep him off it any other day of the week.

The bank agent leaves his vaults in charge of the office-boy, the shopkeeper leaves his customers to the care of his wife, the doctor risks the relapsing of his patients, and the dominie, disdainful of the censure of the School Board proclaims a holiday. If besoms or brooms of the *planta genista* - badge of a royal line – are not to be had conveniently, then the housewife's esparto carpet-switch is surreptitiously conveyed, and the manhood of the village empties

itself on the ice. A frost is elusive and evanescent in these later years, so little time is lost that can be utilised on the pond. The 'hoggs' are birling gaily down the rink long ere it is yet noon, they are still birling when the sun is over the western hills, and the handles are still on them when the dark is down on the glen and a lantern-light marks the tee whereat the players aim with a mechanical precision born of a long day's practice.

To an unimpassioned or superficial observer the scene presented is one of grotesque and misguided emotion. Young men and old, in knickerbockers and Tam-o'-Shanters, dance excitedly between the tees, gesticulating unrestrainedly, sweeping wildly at the ice in front of the gliding stone, and shouting frantically the while. The voracious feature of curling probably accounts for its popular title of the 'roaring game.' A curler has little time for eating, and dinner is a mere convenience to be omitted under the circumstances, but the keen edge of appetite is knocked off hastily on rough 'farls'of oatcake, moistened by reckless – but curiously innocuous – libations of mountain dew. >>>>>>>>>>>>>>>>>*

Should the wind continue from the north, and the waters remain in the grasp of John Frost, the clubs go many miles to meet each other, and compete for the medal of the province, or for simple game. The Highland hotelkeeper, who, in the hot August days took the golden fleece from the Sassenach tourist by the levy of abnormal posting charges, displays quite a different phase in his character by placing his brakes and horses at the free disposal of his brethren of the broom. The master who in summer would grumble at having to let a servant off a day to get married, would hardly dare to refuse him as long a holiday as he liked in curling weather. But the curlers grand contest – the Bisley of the Broom is the Bonspiel, which takes place once a year, if possible under the auspices of the Royal Caledonian Curling Club, whereat curlers from the north of the Forth play those from the south. It is a national event which many a Scottish painter has endeavoured to depict on canvas, but the riot and delight, the abandon and uproar of it, are beyond pigment. To strike the players of a national bonspiel returning home is an experience in festivity and al fresco hospitality calculated to have the most deleterious effects on the system.

RCCC Annual 1893-94

* >>>>>>> *indicates part of text omitted for this publication – Ed.*

Kirriemuir Herald 9th February 1967
EXCITING GAME IN KIRRIE FIXTURES

The second game of the Kirriemuir Curling Club League took place at Dundee last Thursday when Bill Lee's rink overcame Ian Ewart's team 15-6. A slight mishap occurred during the game when Bill Lees slipped and got a nasty crack on the back of his head. Someone was heard to remark that it was "gie hard" but whether this was the ice or Bill's head was not clear. It was maybe coincidental, but Bill's game improved immediately thereafter, and Ian's team not enjoying the best of luck were struggling throughout.

A Curlers Address to 'John Frost'

What ails you at us noo John?
Ye're never seen ava,
Else but a cranreuch* cloak ye don,
Or whyles a shower o'snaw.

I fear ye will your prestige tyne,
Wi' Curlers ane and a',
Unless you come, as in 'Land syne,
In icy garments braw.

Assert your richts amang the saints,
And shake you hoary head,
Declare the Curlers' sad complaints,
Demanding prompt remead.

Your very best it maun be dune,
In lochs o' glassy ice,
So summon a' the powers abune,
And gie them your advice.

Say, that your richts hae been neglectit,
Which winna do ava;
That Curlers aye in hope expectit,
Their winter's frost and snaw.

Then curlers keen will a' rejoice,
To gain what noo seems lost;
And, gladly sing wi' joyous voice,
Hurrah! for auld John Frost.

* cranreuch - hoarfrost

Sir Colin Campbell C.C. Glasgow Nov. 3 1874

Global warming 1874 style! – Ed.

Kirriemuir Herald
22nd February 1968
OUTSIDE EXPERIENCE TELLS

Despite the counter attractions at Tannadice* and Dens Park* last Saturday, Kirriemuir and Cortachy Curling Clubs managed to get the game for the Glasswell Trophy played off. The Dundee cup-tie proved too big an attraction for some and Kirrie was forced to recruit two ladies to make up their team. Let it be said straight away that this in no way weakened their side for they proved to be as good at adapting themselves to the conditions as any. After those in the Kirrie rinks, who had never played on outdoor ice before, had been assured that all they had to do if the ice gave way was to hold their brooms high above their heads till fished out, the game got under way. It was soon obvious that the Cortachy men, who have been playing outside for the past week or two were better up to the conditions than their opponents. Their stones seemed to run better than the Kirrie ones which had been lying unused since the match was last played three years ago.

Adam Whyte's rink of Jim Moffat, Mary Moffat and Alice Ogilvie succeeded in winning five of the ten ends played, but Adam was disappointed at his own inability to master the conditions at his first attempt on outdoor ice, and finally lost 11-5 to Arch. Shaw's rink.

Dave Ewart's rink of John McElwee, Bunt Ewart and Willie Mills fared no better, going down 15-4 to a rink competently skipped by Will Stewart jnr.

Eric Durston, the donor of the cup was unable to be present to present the trophy, but it was duly handed over to the winning skips on the strict understanding that it is only on loan till next year when Kirrie hope to win it back. A most enjoyable afternoon was rounded off with refreshments and sandwiches.

There's no doubt that curling was really meant to be played in such ideal surroundings as was enjoyed at Cortachy. The sun shone all afternoon, and although it may have been a bit warmer in an indoor ice rink, there is nothing to beat the sound of the stone "singing" its way over the pond. The ice may be a bit bumpy, but the conditions are the same for all, and the spectators up on the roadway can vouch from the shouts and laughter which rose from the ice during the afternoon that all the participants were thoroughly enjoying themselves.

* Football Stadiums in Dundee

Robert Burns and Curling

Tam Samson's Elegy

Robert Burns

Verse 4.

When winter muffles up his cloak,
And binds the mire just like a rock;
When to the loughs the curlers flock,
Wi' gleesome speed,
Wha will they station at the cock? –
Tam Samson's dead!

Verse 5.

He was the king of a' the core
To guard or draw, or wick a bore
Or up the rink like Jehu roar
In time o' need;
But now he lags on Death's hog-score
Tam Samson' dead!

Editor's Note

John Syme, a friend of Robert Burns, in a letter dated 5th January 1789 writes 'I have been once or twice in company with Burns, and admire him much…… I missed a meeting with him last Friday at Dumfries, where he played a Bonespeel with the curlers there, and enlivened their Beef and Kail and Tody till the small hours of Saturday morning.'

Kirrriemuir Free Press
14th November 1968
CORTACHY CURLERS HOLD DINNER
First For Lengthy Period

For the first time for a lengthy period Cortachy Curling Club held a dinner this year. It took place at the Royal Jubillee Arms Hotel, Dykehead last Friday night. Mr. David Wardhaugh was "My Lord" while Mr. C. Norrie acted as "My Lord's Officer."

"Cortachy Curling Club" was toasted by Mr. W. McK Irvine and Mr. Wm. Gibson, president, replied. Mr. David Laird proposed the toast of "My Lord and his Officer" to which Mr. Wardhaugh responded.

The toast to "Neighbouring Clubs" was given by Mr. G.W. Neilson, and in this instance, Mr. Wardhaugh made suitable reply. No fewer than a dozen were initiated as members, and they were addressed by Mr. Archie Shaw, the reply being made by Cameron McKiddie. After a delightful meal, musical entertainment was provided by Mr. D. Davidson (accordionist) and Mr. H. Edwards (guitarist.)

Editor 'made' 8/11/68

Laughter from The Ladies

Tune - 'A Wee Doch and Doris"

Just a wee stone a slidin',
Doon a wee sheet of ice.
Just a wee broom a sweepin',
Tae bring it in real nice.
There's a wee skip a-waitin',
At the end of the rink,
And if we don't get it in for shot this time,
Then she'll no' buy a drink.

Scottish Lady Curlers

Tune - 'Clementine

Sister Curlers, Sister Curlers,
Come to see us from o'er the sea.
Pleased to meet you, and to greet you,
Happy here we hope you'll be.

Curling madly, never badly,
Hope that you'll enjoy your stay,
And the friendship made in Scotland,
Brought you back again today.

We're a happy gang of Curlers,
We're the girls that throw the rock,
And it takes a bit of muscle,
And some skill which we've all got.

Tune - 'My Bonnie lies over the Ocean'

I'm really not much of a sweeper,
I haven't an eye for the broom;.
My judgement of weight is just hopeless,
But I throw those stones down with a zoom.

Chorus

Give back, give back, O give back some good curlers to me, to me,
Give back, give back, O give back some good curlers to me.

The lead is a terrible curler!
The third is a sight for the gods!
The second's an absolute washout!
Whose rinks are the good curlers on?

The skipper is wide on her inturns,
She misses the broom by a yard,
She's often just short of the hog line,
When Lord knows she needs a good guard.

Please sweep her stones over the hog line,
Then sweep her stones onto the tee;
Then throw up a guard when they get there,
And send back a winner to me.

I want to say kindly but firmly,
To the nitwits who fixed up this draw,
The gang that I drew down as curlers,
Are the worst that the world ever saw.

Obviously written by a woman about women

And in similar tone to Clementine

Chorus

I'm a curler, I'm a curler,
I'm a curler till I die,
And I'd rather be a curler,
Than at home a-baking pie.

I'm a **lead,** I'm a **lead**,
And I'm always in the know,
If they'd let me skip the game,
Then we'd win for sure I know.

Chorus

I'm a **second**, I'm a **second**,
And I'm never on the broom,
But when it comes to fun and dancing,
I'm the best one in the room.

Chorus

I'm a **third**, I'm a **third**,
And I've often wondered why,
But I'll always be a third
'Til' I learn to yell and lie.

Chorus

I'm a **Skip**, I'm a **Skip**,
And I always get the blame,
But when the team is winning
Then I never hear my name.

13th Aberdeen Ladies Invitation 1999

The Curlers.

Eglinton Flushes Feb. 2ᵈ 1860

Curling Match at Eglinton Castle, Ayrshire 1860
Showing that the fairer sex were early exponents of curling and
how well they used the broom! - Ed

Tune - 'Hello Dolly'

Hello Curlers,

Oh Hello Curlers,

It's so nice to have you here in Aberdeen.

You're curling well curlers,

Looking swell, curlers,

You're still sliding, stones are gliding

And you're having fun.

How's your skip, curlers?

A real drip curlers?

Is she really sweet or is she kind of mean?

Sooooooooooooooooooooo

Throw your stones curlers,

Never mind the aching bones curlers,

Your skip won't love you anyhow,

You're skip won't love you anyhow,

Your skip won't love you anyhow.

13th Aberdeen Ladies Invitation 1999

Tune - 'Are you Lonesome Tonight'

Are you lonesome tonight?

Are your corsets too tight?

Is your bra' breaking apart?

Do you have a big chest?

That makes holes in your vest.

Does your spare tyre reach up to your heart?

Are your stockings all laddered?

Are your shoes wearing thin?

Do you hold up your knickers with a big safety pin?

Are your wallies all worn?

Do they slip when you yawn?

No bloody wonder you're lonesome tonight!!

KIRRIEMUIR HERALD 28TH NOVEMBER 1968

On Monday this week, fortune was kind to Kirrie for a change. They won or "stole" might be a better word, a game against Kirrie Ladies in the Angus province League by 12-10. This was an excellent game in which the ladies excelled as they always do against Kirrie. Isa Pate's team of Mary Moffat, Isobel Dunn and Cathie McIldowie played excellently on the fast ice and although down 4-1 soon after the start, fought back to lead 7-4 and then 10-8. The Kirrie skip who will be nameless, had one of these evenings when everything came off, but he had two outrageous flukes to steal the game in its latter stages. He was supported by Cameron McKiddie, Jim Moffat and Spence Yeaman, who voted it one of the most exciting games they had taken part in.

Fund Raising Frolics

Blooming good salesmen ready to go

Jumping for joy at the sales

WHAT A BLOOMING BARGAIN!

LOCALLY GROWN DAFFODIL BULBS OF INTERNATIONAL QUALITY

5 KILO. BAG £3.00
10 KILO. BAG £5.00

During autumn 2007 & 2008 members took a stall at Angus Farmers' Markets held monthly in Forfar & Montrose selling daffodil bulbs and photo greeting cards gifted by two of their members.

Their aggressive but humorous sales technique was very successful raising almost £2500 towards the Bicentenary Fund

FOR SALE

LOCALLY GROWN DAFFODIL BULBS OF INTERNATIONAL QUALITY

GREAT VALUE
5 KILO. BAG £3.00
10 KILO. BAG £5.00

PLANT BETWEEN AUGUST - END OCTOBER

KIRRIEMUIR CURLING CLUB BICENTENARY 2009

David Urquhart's novel way of delivering daffodil bags

James Upton looks on as Bill Keillor(L) & Cameron McKiddie brush up their sales pitch

'Croupier', John Duncan takes the bets at Blackjack

James Arnott &
Cameron McKiddie prepare

An excited capacity. crowd of 180 attended KCC's Casino Night in Kirriemuir Town Hall on 13th April 2007.

Playing Roulette, Blackjack and Chuck-a-Luck the crowd soon got that Las Vegas enthrallment as they waited for the spin of the wheel, the turn of the card, the throw of the dice.

"Place your bets" - Roulette

The barmen are kept busy

A Nicht Wi' The Kirrie Curlers

My Lord, ye ha'e asked me a story to tell,
And your word I'll ne're try to gainsay;
For to me it is clear, as a curler, keen, here,
My skip's orders I ever obey.

So I'll try to sweep clean frae my mind a' that's been
Perturbin' it durin' the day;
And my spavied Pegasus I'll spur up Parnasaus,
Though foonder she should on the brae.

Nae subject I'll tak' frae the hackneyed auld pack
O' classical books on the shel's;
My subject shall be –juist the folks that I see;
In short, I will speak o' oorsel's.

My Lord's an M.B. wha won his degree
In Rothesay Soci'ty, he claims;
A descendant is he o' Wallace, the free,   (1).
Wha "checked" England's "overdraft" aims.

We've a lively "L.G.", though nae statesman is he;
My Lord's Officer is he to-night;
He's noted for readiness, famed for his steadiness
On a white line along the High "Strite".

Oor Scribe, I may say, will each curler "survey",
For guid "metal" he's aye sweer to lose;
And though rust should debar you, he'll find means to "tar" you,
And "chip" you when late wi' your dues.

Parson Erchie noo scan; he's oor medicine man;
Rare spirit to "babies" gi'es he;
And should they but froon, he comforts each loon,
And wipes the "saut" tear from his e'e.

CURLING ON A CRAMPET ON KINNORDY LOCH? IN THE 1930s?

From L.to R.   David McKiddie, Rev_____, _____,_____, David Smith, Jim Annand

A bevy for a bevy of beauties at Cortachy pond 1979
Eunice McKiddie, Judith Dorman, Ann Herd

To hear ye your orison, here's Harry Rorison –   (2)
A sportsman that Kirrie lo'es weel –
In hert he's aye lichtsome, but see'm in an Eichtsome,
'Twad mak' e'en the steadiest "reel".

O' icemesters three around us I see;
And each at his job is a don;
Dick Lockhart is ane – wha to bool aye is fain –
O' the ithers I'll speak later on.

O' Mackenzies we've twa – Jack and Jim – nane ava' (3)
Mair skilled than that pair at the "pen";
Famed for mutton that's cheap – great men amang sheep
--But nane o' them sheep amang men.

Though maybe the auldest that curls on the ice,
Jim Brow's still at he'rt a young chap;
He's wi' "Craigies" the nicht, keepin' young curlers richt,
Though they'd baith raither been at the Nap.

At Jack Mack's direction, "pot lids" to perfection
Or a "wick" that comes gently in-by;
Or a "fly-cast" for sport, to fill up a port,
The man frae Dean Hoose can supply.

Jim Stewart's turned out, defyin' the gout,   (4)
A skip in great victories rife;
Till an auld Farfar loon left him thirty shots doon;
And proved quite the "bain" o' Jim's life.

There's a dentist that aims aye for plums in his pies, (5)
Like little Jack Horner sae braw;
He should be I think, a great man in a rink,
For he's very weel up in the "draw".

Jim Lindsay is here; a lad o' guid cheer,   (6)
And worthy his "pla(i)ce" by his looks;
And if he should fail by guid play to prevail,
He'll "flounder" in somehow by "flukes".

**Cortachy & Kirriemuir Clubs playing for the Glasswell Cup
On Loch Heath, Glen Clova 2002**

For "short-cuts" to the pin, by a "close shave" to win,   (7)
I'll say to Jim Annand commend me;
But to "butcher" this stane or "put that oot o' pain"
For that, Donald Scott I wad send ye.

Noo, Will Irvine, there, is a paradox fair,   (8)
Amang sheep he's continually joggin';
But gi'e him a stane and juist leave him alane,
And he'll never be guilty o "Hoggin".

As guid as a doctor's oor freend Charlie Proctor,   (9)
His singin' sae raises the spirit;
While his pal, the Toon Clark, finds it michty hard wark (10)
Some sense frae his Coondil to ferret.

Notice, tae, Young "Drumclune", a cheery-gaun loon'   (11)
And a fermer o' promise beside;
They tell me he'll daur grow craps oot o' glaur
Afore he's been lang in Lochside.

Jim Osler, I've seen 'e; your smile's worth a guinea;   (12)
A better chiel' Kirrie ne'er seeks;
Wi' the ice in fine trim, ye can aye lippen Jim
To put on opponents "the breeks"

There's a chap from Dunbog amang us incog.   (13)
Though it's kent that Sam Pate is his name;
Noo settled at Reedie, you'll find that he'll lead ye
To vict'ry abroad or at hame.

APRES CURLING ON CORTACHY POND CIRCA 1978-79
L to R. Dave Black, Hugh Hood, Dave Torrie, Bob Robertson, John Baynes,
Gordon Ager, Cameron McKiddie, Dudley Dorman

Frae the clubs roond aboot ye've a fair turnout,   (14)
For they ne'er like a treat to be lost;
And they ken they can lay on the best usoqubae
When ye've chartered John Scott as your host.

This Baronet smart is the Laird o' Lindertis;   (15)
We'll drink to his health if we may,
And the lass he has chosen frae bonnie Glenprosen
To walk by his side in the way.

Some great lads, I daresay are doon here frae Pearsie –
Will Lamond wham bogles treat rough –
And I fairly could deave ' e wi' tales o' "Ascreavie"
Wha clears oot a heid like a snuff.

At Pearsie a'e nicht, wi' the mune shinin' bricht,
He delivered a stane in some vagary
It gaed clean throo the heid and ne're slackened speed
Till it cam' to the doorstep o' Ba'gray.

But was it Tam's strength that sent it that length,
And brocht it to Ba'gray door skiddin'?
I'm certain, for ane, 'twas a musical stane,
That was drawn there by Dave Whamond's fiddlin'.

Dave's absent, I see, but great fiddlers three
I notice as roond me I glance;
They detest the jazz craze, but in reels and Strathspeys,
They've the jerk that compels ye to dance.

Jim Cameron, see! for a champion he   (16)
At festivals mony, I trow;
While Alick Bain patch could a fiddle frae matchwood
An' "Kina'ty's" far-famed for the bow.

And ye will confess, sir, oor freend the "Professor",
Wha by the piano is set,
Has only to be wi' thae great fiddlers three
To complete the maist perfect quartette.

Nereby's "Sandy Eck" wha has made a lang trek
To be ane o' this company free;
A true sport is Sandy, wi' rod and gun handy;
And great at the gralloch is he.

Then frae fair Downiepark there's a lad here I mark –
He's Donald Macdonald, you know;
He's a lad wi' few fauts though to parsons and rats
He' declared a most dangerous foe.

This nicht half a score ha'e come to your door
Frae a place that they ca' Brochty Ferry;
And a cheerier crew I'm sure ye ne'er knew
To invade the douce precincts o' Kirrie.

If they need introduction, my only production   (17)
Is ane that, my Lord, ye'll rely on;
It's that ilk mother's son an entry had won
As a personal pal o' "Chay" Lyon.

54

There's Colin ye ken as the blithest o' men;
Mony a nicht in this toon he's made bright,
And hooe'er things may gang we can ne'er a' be wrang,
For "Lang Willie" will always be "Wright".

There's Fred ye'll hear singin'; Jim Low we were bringin'
To be "made" in his ain native toon;
Donald Ross, if you please, is a dab at the keys
And can keep <u>maist</u> o' <u>folk</u> in guid tune.

'Twad need juist a Raeburn to picter Dave Laburn
When he's at his best on the ice;
"Dodo" Redford's a chiel' ye will learn to like weel,
and "Pitairlie" kens every device.

My Lord, if at closin' the Room's hard to clear
And in vain on the table ye bang –
Here's the best way of a' to shoo awa' –
Get Jim Wilson to sing them a sang.

O' the last o' the batch ye can noo tak' a "swatch" –
O' failin's I ken he has mony
And but twae virtues sweet – he's nae hyprocite,
And he aye tries to stand by a cronie.

Geo. Broon is a jewel at gi'en young lads gruel;   (18)
There's a "Farmer" that's aye in a "Sosh"
Hugh Black whase fine voice mak's the saddest rejoice
And "Whitey" frae Clova – by Gosh!   (19)

Oor "New Brooms" ye've seen. Lets hope they "Sweep clean"
And get a guid "grip" o' the game;
Frae a'airts they've come to the "Channel Stane's" hum.
And we've tried hard to "mak'" them at hame.

There's Roy, the Inspector, wha I wad expect, sir,
To "lock up" the "secrets" wi' zest;
And a colleague retired a' Kirrie admired ---
Bob Stormont o' Sergeants the best.   (20)

There's an engineer laddie frae far Irrawadi
And a "P.C." that's not on "the Force"
O' Carnegies there's Brewster, the pike-fishing booster, (21)
And a great many others, of course!

To a' thae young gentry we've gi'en a soft entry
The Myst'ries o' curlin'into;
But they'd better tak' care o' loose tongues to beware
And to keep a' the promises true.

55

Or that "Alchemist" chiel' wha raised up the de'il (22)
Will get on their track in a hurry
And wi' nae parson by "Cloutie's" wrath to defy
They will find that they've guid cause to worry.

Your president's absence I greatly regret
For langest he's been in the Club,
And acknowledge ye can that <u>there</u> is a man
O' a' Kirrie's int'rests the hub.
An ancestor bold, in the brave days of old,
Saved the life o' oor land's naval chief,
And if law pleas should plague ye, to John A. Carnegie
You're wise if ye gang wi' your brief.

Sir Torquil an a' is missin' Bob Law
Wi his stories as strong as himsel'
And I'm vexed "Hayston's" cauld has kept frae oor fauld
Ane itherwise soond as a bell.

Noo, my Lord, I maun close my epistle jocose,
I admit it's been lackin'in sense;
But in spirit o' fun everything has been done
And I trust it has gi'en nae offence.

J. Robertson Coupar   5th December 1932

56

Wallace Neilson & Editor were able to identify the name & occupation of some of those present.

(1)	M.B. Wallace	Banker
(2)	Harry Rorison	Scottish Episcopal minister
(3)	James & John MacKenzie	Shepherds
(4)	J.C.Stewart	Dairyman
(5)	---------------	Dentist
(6)	Jim Lindsay	Fishmonger
(7	James R. Annand	Gents & Ladies Hairdresser @ 22, Bank Street, K.
(8	Will Irvine	Sheep farmer
(9)	Charlie Proctor	Town Chamberlain possibly
(10)	David Smith	Solicitor & Town Clark
(11)	Will Wyllie	Farmer at Drumclune
(12)	Jim Osler	Gent's Outfitter, Narrow Roods
(13)	Sam Pate	Farmer at Reedie
(14)	J. M. Scott	Hotel Proprietor
(15)	Sir Torquil	Munro Estate Owner
(16)	Jim Cameron	Lemonade Manufacturer & Band leader
(17)	Charles Lyon	Ironmonger
(18)	Geo Brown	Jeweller
(19)	Archie Whyte	Sheep farmer at the Spot, Glenprosen
(20)	Bob Stormont	Police Sergeant
(21)	Brewster Carnegie	Lawyer
(22)	David McKiddie	Pharmacist

Every picture tells a story - 3

Jim Strathearn, a regular Kirrie curler is renowned for his weighty demolition shots, and usually very effective in removing a barrel-load of stones in one go. However an audible warning should be given prior to his attempt so that those curlers on his own and adjacent rinks can take cover. In 1983 as his 40th birthday approached, Kirrie artist Joyce Grubb undertook to produce a painting of Jim in action from my very rough sketch. Jim is unmistakeable in his customary bonnet and other notable curlers are easily identifiable. Clockwise from Jim are Brian Mollison, Lindsay Brown, Iain Grubb, Dudley Dorman, Cameron McKiddie, Roy Davidson, Jim Smith and Drummond Herd. Jim was thrilled with his birthday present.

Joyce had cooked up a corker and therefore it was appropriate that my payment to her for producing this 'masterpiece' was a large Cavalcade electric oven, which our new kitchen had made redundant.

It would be amiss of me, a native of Kirriemuir, not to include references to curling from the pen of Kirriemuir's most famous son, Sir J.M.Barrie (Author of 'Peter Pan') whose birthplace is but a skip and a jump from my own front gate.

An extract from 'The Little Minister by Sir J.M.Barrie

>>>> A black frost had set in, and one walking on the glen road could imagine that through the cracks in it he saw a loch glistening. From my door I could hear the roar of curling stones at Rashie-bog, which is almost four miles nearer Thrums. On the day I am recalling, I see that I made only one entry in my diary, "At last bought Waster Lunny's bantams." Well do I remember the transaction, and no wonder, for I had all but bought the bantams every day for a six months.

About noon the doctor's dog cart was observed by all the Tenements standing at the Auld Licht manse. The various surmises were wrong. Margaret had not been taken suddenly ill; Jean had not swallowed a darning-needle; the minister had not walked out at his study window in a moment of sublime thought. Gavin stepped into the dog cart, which at once drove off in the direction of Rashie-bog, but equally in error were those who said that the doctor was making a curler of him. >>>>*

"You want me to go with you?"

Spoken by the minister

"Yes, though I must warn you it may be a distressing scene; indeed, the truth is that I am loth to face Nanny alone today. Mr. Duthie should have accompanied me, for the Websters are Established Kirk; ay, and so he would if Rashie-bog had not been bearing. A terrible snare this curling, Mr. Dishart" – here the doctor sighed – "I have known Mr. Duthie wait until midnight struck on Sabbath, and then off to Rashie-bog with a torch." >>>>*

"Why are we not going up the Roods?" he asked.   *Spoken by the minister*

"Well," said the doctor slowly, "at the top of the Roods there is a stance for the circuses, and this old beast of mine won't pass it. You know unless you are behind the clashes and clavers of Thrums, that I bought her from the manager of a travelling

show. She was the horse('Lightning' they called her) that galloped round the ring at a mile an hour, and so at the top of the Roods she is still unmanageable. She once dragged me to the scene of her former triumphs, and went revolving round it, dragging the machine after her."

"If you had not explained that," said Gavin, I might have thought that you wanted me to pass by Rashie bog."

The doctor, indeed, was already standing up to catch a first glimpse of the curlers.

"Well," he admitted, "I might have managed to pass the circus ring, though what I have told you is true. However, I have not come this way merely to see how the match is going. I want to shame Mr. Duthie for neglecting his duty. It will help me to do mine, for the Lord knows I am finding it hard, with the music of those stones in my ears."

"I have never seen it played before," Gavin said, standing up in his turn. "What a din they make! McQueen, I believe they are fighting!"

"No, no, said the excited doctor, "they are just a bit daft. That's the proper spirit for the game. Look, that's the baron-baillie near standing on his head, and there's Mr. Duthie off his head a' thegither. Yon' twa weavers and a mason cursing the laird and the man wi' the besom is the Master of Crumnathie."

"A democracy, at all events," said Gavin.

"By no means," said the doctor, "it's an aristocracy of intellect. Gee up, Lightning, or the frost will be gone before we get there."

"It is my opinion, doctor," said Gavin, "that you will have bones to set before that game is finished. I can see nothing but legs now."

"Don't say a word against curling, sir, to me," said McQueen, whom the sight of a game in which he must not play had turned crusty.

"Dangerous! It's the best medicine I know of. Look at that man coming across the field. It is Jo Strachan. Well, sir, curling saved Jo's life after I had given him up. You don't believe me? Hie Jo, Jo Strachan, come here and tell the minister how curling put you on your legs again."

Strachan came forward, a tough little, wizened man, with red flannel round his ears to keep out the cold.

"It's gospel what the doctor says, Mr. Dishart," he declared. "Me and my brither Sandy was baith ill, and in the same bed, and the doctor had hopes o'Sandy, but nane o'me. Ay. weel, when I heard that, I thocht I micht as weel die on the ice as in my bed, so I was up and on wi' my claethes. Sandy was mad at me, for he was no curler, and he says, 'Jo Strachan, if you gang to Rashie-bog, you'll assuredly be brought home a corp,' I didna heed him, though, and off I gaed."

"And I see you did not die," said Gavin.

"No me," answered the fish cadger, with a grin. "Na, but the joke o't is, it was Sandy that died."

"Not the joke, Jo," corrected the doctor, "the moral."

"Ay, the moral; I'm aye forgetting the word."

McQueen, enjoying Gavin's discomfiture, turned Lightning down the Rashie-bog road, which would be impassable as soon as the thaw came. In summer Rashie-bog is several fields in which a cart does not sink unless it stands still, but in winter it is a loch with here and there a spring where dead men are said to lie. There are no rushes at its east end, and here the dog-cart drew up near the curlers, a crowd of men dancing, screaming, shaking their fists and sweeping, while half a hundred onlookers got in their way gesticulating and advising.

"Hold me tight." Doctor whispered to Gavin," or I'll be leaving you to drive Nanny to the poorhouse by yourself."

He had no sooner said this than he tried to jump out of the trap.

"You donnert fule, John Robbie," he shouted to a player, "soop her up, man, soop her up; no. no dinna, dinna: leave her alane. Baillie, leave her alane, you blazing idiot. Mr. Dishart, let me go; what do you mean, sir, by hanging on to my coat tails? Dang it all, Duthie's winning. He has it, he has it!"

"You're to play, doctor?" some cried, running to the dog-cart. "We hae missed you sair."

"Jeames, I—I---. No, I daurna."

"Then we'll get our licks. I never saw the minister in sic form. We can do nothing against him."

"Then,"cried McQueen, "I'll play, Come what will, I'll play. Let go my tails, Mr. Dishart, or I'll cut them off. Duty? Fiddlesticks!"

"Shame on you sir," said Gavin; "yes, and on you others who would entice him from his duty."

"Shame!" the doctor cried. "Look at Mr. Duthie. Is he ashamed? And yet the man has been reproving me for twelvemonths because I've refused to become one of his elders. Duthie," he shouted, "think shame on yourself for curling this day."

Mr. Duthie had carefully turned his back on the trap, for Gavin's presence in it annoyed him. We seldom care to be reminded of our duty by seeing another do it. Now, however he advanced to the dog-cart, taking the far side of Gavin.

"Put on your coat, Mr. Duthie." said the doctor," and come with me to Nanny Webster's. You promised."

Mr Duthie looked quizzically at Gavin and then at the sky.

"The thaw may come at any moment," he said.

"I think the frost is to hold," said Gavin.

"It may hold over tomorrow," Mr. Duthie admitted: "but tomorrow's the Sabbath, and so a lost day."

"A what?" exclaimed Gavin, horrified.

"I only mean," Mr. Duthie answered colouring, "that we can't curl on the Lord's day. As for what it may be like on Monday, no one can say. No. doctor, I won't risk it. We're in the middle of a game, man."

Gavin looked very grave.

"I see what you are thinking, Mr. Dishart," the old minister said doggedly ; "but then, you don't curl. You are very wise. I have forbidden my sons to curl."

"Then you openly snap your fingers at your duty, Mr. Duthie?" said the doctor, loftily. ("You can let go my tails now, Mr. Dishart, for the madness has passed.")

"None of your virtuous airs, McQueen," said Mr. Duthie, hotly. "What was the name of the doctor who warned women never to have bairns while it was hauding?"

"And what," retorted McQueen, "was the name of the minister that told his session he would neither preach or pray while the black frost lasted?"

"Hoots, doctor," said Duthie, "Don't lose your temper because I'm in such form."

"Don't lose yours, Duthie, because I aye beat you."

"You beat me, McQueen! Go home, sir, and don't talk havers. Who beat you at-"

"Who made you sing small at---"

"Who won----"

"Who---"

"Who---"

"I'll play you on Monday for whatever you like!" shrieked the doctor.

"If it holds," cried the minister, "I'll be here the whole day. Name the stakes yourself. A stone?"

"No," the doctor said, "but I'll tell you what we'll play for. You've been dinging me doited about that eldership, and we'll play for't. If you win I accept office."

"Done," said the minister, recklessly.

The dog-cart was now turned towards Windyghoul, its driver once more good-humoured, but Gavin silent.

"You would have been better of my deaf ear just now, Mr. Dishart," McQueen said, after the loch had been left behind. "Aye, and I'm thinking my pipe would soothe you. But don't take it so much to heart, man. I'll lick him easily. He's a decent man, the minister, but vain of his play, ridiculously vain. However, I think the sight of you, in the place that should have been his, has broken his nerve for this day, and our side may win yet."

"I believe," Gaven said with sudden enlightenment, "that you brought me here for that purpose."

"Maybe," chuckled the doctor; "maybe." Then he changed the subject suddenly. "Mr. Dishart," he asked, "were you ever in love?"

"Never!" answered Gavin violently.

"Well, well, "said the doctor, "don't terrify the horse. I have been in love myself. It's bad, but it's nothing to the curling.

>> Some parts of the story omitted – Ed

61

Ye may bounce ower your billiards

Ye may bounce ower your billiards, grow great ower yer gowf,
Or craw* crouse* ower yer cribbage in some coie howf*;
Ye may whimper for whist, an' for loo* ye may grane,
But for me let me curl wi' the aul' channel stane.
In cauld winter, when hoary king Frost reigns supreme,
An' has silenced the sang o' ilk burnie and stream;
When the bauld babblin' brook has nae story to tell,
Let me aff an' awa' tae the pond at Rozelle.

There the whirr o' the stane an' the whisk o' the cowe*,
An' the jokes an' the shouts set my heart in a lowe*;
It's a potion, a tonic, a cure for a' ills--
Dr John Frost, believe me, supplies the best pills.
Hear the Skip shouting winningly, 'Lay me ane there;
Noo jist ower the collie*, I'm wantin' nae mair;
Noo watch her noo, nurse noo boys help her a wee;
Weel play'd, sir! weel play'd, sir! she's ower, let her dee.

What words half sae cheering, 'It's a perfect pat lid;'
Or,' Man, you for a player, but losh, it's ower gude.'
'A great shot, sir! great shot sir!' rings ower the pond:
'You play like a book, sir!' the echoes resound.
'Tak an inwick on that or an outwick on this;
Noo mak sure o' yer stane, I don't want ye to miss.'
An' to do it, what pleasure, a kingdom is won,
When 'Hoora!' shouts the Skip, 'you have play'd it, my son.'

Yes, gae bounce ower billiards, grow great ower yer gowf,
Or craw crouse ower cribbage in some cosie howf;
Ye may whimper for whist, an' for loo ye may grane,
But let me to Rozelle wi' the aul' channel stane.

AYR November 1874

RCCC Annual 1877

*craw - call * crouse – lively * howf - haunt * loo - old card game*

* cowe - broom * lowe - blaze * collie - hog line*

**When all is done,
And you have won,
Don't head straight for your car.
Those defeated,
Should be treated
To a drink up at the bar.**

Anon.

Press Reports

Kirriemuir Free Press 14th January 1971
ANNUAL CURLING CHALLENGE MATCH – Excitement All The Way

The annual challenge match of three rinks between Forfar and Kirriemuir clubs for the Stewart Tankard took place at Dundee Ice Rink last Thursday. It proved a cliffhanger until the last two stones were delivered. Jim Smith's rink of Alex Ogilvie, Chick Wilson and Jack Ewart had fought a losing battle all the way against Bill Duff and went down 15-8. Ian Ewart's team, comprising Jim Moffat, Alan Bruce and Ed Weighton, who were trailing 8-1 against George Smith, at one stage fought back to 9-7, and were lying shot at the last end with Smith's last stone to come. He played a masterly shot and edged off the Kirrie stone for shot, and a 10-7 win instead of a 9-8 result Kirrie had counted on. This meant three up to Forfar instead of one and with the first two rinks decided, Kirrie were down 10 shots over all. Despite this, Kirrie had high hopes of victory for with two ends to go Bruce Paul's rink of Adam Whyte, Mary Moffat(sub) and Cameron McKiddie were leading 20-6 against the redoubtable Sid Jarvis. It was when he realised that all depended on him that Sid showed what a grand curler he is. Never flustered, never hurried, he took three shots at the second last end and at the last was lying three with Bruce to play the final stone. It must be difficult playing when you know that the overall state of the game was 35 for Kirrie and 34 for Forfar, and as the opposition was lying three shots, which would give them victory, you had to do something spectacular with the last stone. Bruce tried to draw the shot, but a Forfar stone was strategically placed by the wily Sid right in the draw, and Bruce unfortunately popped it in for another shot to Forfar to make the final score 38 for Forfar and 35 to Kirrie. Another year before Kirrie can wrest that trophy from Forfar's grasp, but if next year's players show the same determination for Kirrie, they may yet do.

Kirriemuir Free Press - *25th November 1971*
CURLERS COMPETE IN POINTS CONTEST
Lady Proves Winner

Maybe it was the weather, but there was a poor turnout of members when the annual points competition of Kirriemuir Curling Club was held at Dundee on Tuesday night.>>>To make up their numbers, the Kirrie club invited Jessma Lindsay and Isobel Dunn of Kirrie ladies as both had expressed a desire to participate in such a competition. For the uninitiated, each player is playing for himself and the object is to demonstrate one's skill in the basic arts of the game – striking, drawing, guarding, promoting and so on. Douglas Gourlay once again ran out winner, with 19 points – a poor score for this individual – and was "chased" home by Jim Moffat with 18. >>> Jessma Lindsay, who had come along "just to see how it was done" shattered the men by scoring 21, and Isobel Dunn who arrived late, and missed her favourite shot – that of striking at which she would surely have picked up four points out of eight, finished with 16.

>>> *Only pertinent parts of report included*

Interview with Wallace Neilson

by Cameron McKiddie 11th April 2006

Today I am interviewing Wallace Neilson, who is the oldest surviving past member of Kirriemuir Curling Club. During this interview I hope to learn the history of Wallace and in particular record his thoughts and experiences as a curler around Kirriemuir. For the ease of recording this history, a tape-recorder is being used and to loosen the tongues and for us both to enjoy this trip down memory lane, we are to do damage to a newly opened bottle of Wallace's favourite tipple. Wallace, to quote another stalwart of Kirriemuir Curling Club, the late Ian Ewart, one time farmer at Kilnhill, " Your astonishing good health"

Wallace in typical pose

Wallace tell me your full name, your age and when and where you born. What did your parents do, did you have any brothers or sisters?

I'm George Wallace Neilson, a' the letters that comes for me, from the council & a' thing, it's a' George that's on it.

And when were you born?·

Seven, six 1915.

Here that's no bad!

I'll be 91 in June   *(In 2006)*

God you've done well then, so what do you think is the secret then?

Och, I dinna ken – it's no easy kening that, is it Cameron?

And you say you were born across the road here?

Aye. 3, Manse Close.

That whar the car park is now?

Aye.

Were your folks in Kirrie a lang time?

Well, aye fer a guid while, ma father cam from Brechin.

And where did he work at in Kirrie?

He was a tailor, wi' what dae ya ca' him?

No' be Rattray?

Aye it wis Rattray.

(Rattrays – Gents Outfitters at 14 Bank Street)

So he was in there then- you'd be a' richt for a suit then?

Aye, ha, ha, well he wiz a tailor to trade. Then we left there & went up tae the Roods.

So when you were staying over in Manse Lane, did you come to Reform Street school from Manse Lane or did you move before that?

Lottie, ma sister wha's older than me, they were the only two that wiz born in Manse Close, but there was six o' us a' the gether.

So where did you move after that?

Went up tae the Roods, 87 Roods.

Aye I ken whar you are, that wid be on the richt side gaein up afore Stuchie Scots?   *(Stewart Scott)*

Oh past that, ye ken the road into the English church?

Aye. So from there you would have come to Reform Street school?

Oh aye.

Doon the back way, by Rosefield Gardens?

No, no I cam doon the Rids.   *The Roods*

Did yeh? We used to sometimes – we, I was born in Braeholm ....

Aye that's right, whar John Gilmour bides. It wiz funny, I wis just thinking about that ye ken when I was going through... I said Cameron, he used tae bide at the tap of the Rids when I was there aye that's right; near sure that Doctor Gilmour's in that hoose noo.

Dr John Gilmour, member of KCC

That's right, that's whar I was born an' we used to - oh I widna say every day but we used to play fitba' up 'n' doon the Roods 'cos there was hardly ony traffic.

Oh aye I had a braw time when I bade in the Rids -- oot an' in ain another hooses an' a' thing.

Aye it was good fun an' when we were sledging we wid come right doon the Roods, doon the narrow Roods...

Aye we did that, we used to see how far we could get could get up, what dae ya ca' it - Bellies Brae. At that time we used to have a lookout at Whiteside in case the bobbies were aboot. Oh, oor sledges an' that were teen but we aye got them back in the morning.

So did you enjoy your schooling at Reform Street?

Aye at that time you only got up to Jocky Gordons. He was the headmaster, just up tae five then an' then ye hud to gae ower tae the Websters.

(Websters Seminary, now Websters High School)

Oh it was only up to five?   *(primary 5)*

Aye it was only up tae five at Reform Street – when ye went up higher ye went tae the Websters.

So how many brothers and sisters?

Two brothers and three sisters. Actually the twa youngest ones, they were born in the Town Hall.

So now you moved from Manse Lane up to the Roods and then back doon to the Town Hall?

Aye that's right.

So when did you first find out about curling – was it as a young laddie?

No, no the first time, ah'll tell you the year I started curlin' – it was 1948. I'd come back to work in the factory, in the Gairie like, and there was a blacksmith there- Dave Lyall and he was a curler and he got me started.   *(J&D Wilkie Ltd. Gairie*

textile works – chiefly jute products at that time)

So you would have been in your 30's at that time?

Oh aye, aye.

And when you started curling where would that have been then?

Started curlin' up at the Glengate – that was the only curlin' there was.

(An artificial concrete patch just off the Glengate, a street in Kirrie)

There was never any curling on the ponds or on the lochs; or anything like that in your day – it was always at the Glengate?

Oh no we used tae go out tae Cortachy.

(A village up the Glens with a curling pond)

Aye but the Kirrie rink was up the Glengate?

Aye twa rinks.

Would that have been started in the late 30's?

Aye it must have been, it was there afore I was involved. Well what happened, how I started was, well, as I said he was the blacksmith in the factory and he started me. We used to finish at 5 o'clock and we'd go up and spray the rink and then about half past seven or so it was frozen, ye see and nae bother.

So how long did you need to let it lie?

Oh about an hour or so onyway, and by the way ye see that thing about Fishy Allan?

Aye.

It wisn't Fishy Allan, it was Fishy Lindsay.

Fishy Lindsay – of course it was. So there was one in his shop, a blue light?

Aye, a blue licht aye.

(At a time when there would have been few phones, this was an ingenious system of switching on a blue light in the window of Lindsay's fish shop to indicate that curling was available)

So that a'body could just turn the corner – curlin' on the night. So did ye get a lot of curling over the winter?

Oh aye, we used tae get a lot of curlin' there. Ye didna' need an awfa lot ye ken. *(ice)* We just sprayed it a' you see. And it was lucky at that time – och you'll maybe mind, ye ken Willie Mill?

Aye the brickie.

Aye, he was a great curler and he was a great help and if onything happened to the rink he wiz able to ah – aye he was a keen keen curler.

So you had a shed where you stored your stones?

Oh aye.

Did you buy your own stones?

No I never bocht stones.

So there were stones there that you could use?

Yer faither had a pair of stones.

(David McKiddie-Pharmacist at 16, Bank St.)

He would have done but he certainly didna' have any stones by the time I came back and I suspect they were just there among the rest.

Jeemie Annand tae, dae ye mind?

(Barber at 24, Bank Street)

Oh aye.

Aye he hud stanes tae, There was ane or twa of them hud stanes.

So when you went up, first there on the ice? You sorted yourselves oot? And did you have to go through the apprentice of starting as second and then on to lead?

Oh aye aye it was just the same.

And eh it wouldn't be a matter of playing so many ends did it?

Naw ye just played away.

Ye'd played for an hour or two?

Oh aye, oh aye, oh God aye – sometimes it was a lang time.

And would there being sometimes curlin' every day of the week?

Ye could 'ave easily gotten it, aye you could be as lang as it kept frostie enough tae dae it.

What about on a Saturday would you curl during the day at all?

Aye, aye.

Were you allowed to curl on a Sunday?

Naw! Oh no no' on a Sunday. We used to have some braw times up there.

And you'd had lights?

Aye, there was lichts.

Electric lights?

Aye.

And it widna have cost you very much money in these days?

No no no, it didna' cost you much. Ah cannie mind how much it was but it wisna, much.

It had been a noisy wi of daeing up there?

Aye aye.

Did they tak' a bottle up with them? Or..

No, that's one thing I never.....

That whar the Durston Trophy started. Aye, it wiz Eric Durston that gie the cup – you mind of Eric?

Kirriemuir Free Press 6th February 1975
Newcomers perform well in curling contest
Seventeen members turned up for the Kirrie Curling Club's points competition. The cup for this competition is more than one hundred years old and depicts scenes of outdoor curling as it was played in those far off days. Judging by the points scored by the winners at that time, they must have been better curlers than the present day members or maybe they had better ice to play on. Going into the last end, half a dozen players were still in with a chance of lifting this fine trophy and it was good to see newcomers to the competition John Gilmour, David Torrie, Stewart Findlater and Iain Grubb featuring prominently in this group. When the scores were added up, Jack Donaldson emerged the winner, followed one point behind by Cameron McKiddie with John Gilmour and Spence Yeaman joint third.
A good night was enjoyed by all the participants.

Aye, at Glasswell. So that would be, you said you started about 1948?

Aye but it would have been further on than that for the Durston Trophy. I dinna ken how long the Durston Trophy's been on the go.

Ah tell you afore I came over I was actually lookin' through the Annual to find out when -

Wallace Neilson's name first appeared and …em. you were definitely a member in 1952 but I couldn't find any reference to 51 but of course it takes a wee while sometimes to get the names……

Well that whan I started '48 and Eric used tae come up.. that's how at that time it had to be played outside. It was between Cortachy and Kirrie for the Durston Trophy.

So when did you leave school then- 15?

Aye.

And what did you dae when you left school?

This'll surprise ya. I was a bus conductor wi' Meffan.

(James Meffan's buses)

So you were a bus conductor first of all – so did you do that for a while?

Ya see, ah wanted in tae serve ma time in the factory – at that time you hud an awfu' job getting in ye see, hud ma name in but by good luck my grandfather – mind my grandfather had the …bit *(boot)* shop in Bank Street?

(Factory–2 textile works in Kirrie at that time)

Of course.

That was my grandfather – then there was my uncle Jim had it after.

Jim Moncur?

Aye, he was my uncle – my grandfather had it at

that time and he was awfa pallie wi' Smert – that was through the bowling of course. So he comes up ae day says, ye heve tae gae ower an see Mr. Smart – he wants tae see you – I got started right away.

So what did you start as?

A mechanic, aye the trouble was when your time was oot in the factory – ya did yer 5 years and then when

your time was oot you got the kick.

What's your memory of the Second World War?

The Second World War? Ah was never in the army and me being an engineer ya , when your time was oot, tried here and there but a had a pal in Glesga and he wiz in the shipyards so he says come through and you'll get started –so a went awa' through there and that hud been nineteen thirty eight and for a start I was in the shipyard and then we wiz building the battleships and that and the word came oot that the war was going to start an' there was three Farfar boys and a Dundee lad in there and they got the twig – that they were wantin', needin' engineers in the Blackness foundry, so says, what about it, he says we'd be nearer hame onywey ye see. Cos a' o' whar were in digs the same as me ye see. So we gie up an cam' through. We wiz in the Blackness foundry a' the time of the war.

Aye, how long did you have in Glasgow then?

Oh just over a year.

So you came back to Dundee?

Aye, at the Blackness found… and then no' long efter that the war did start.

So did you stay in Dundee at that time?

Well, when a started first, a hud tae tak digs in Dundee and then they put in a nicht shift, so I put in for nicht shift so I could go back and forward. Then you were workin' twelve hoors a day at that time.

Were you still biding up the Roods then?

No, no I wiz married be that time – I was married in 1942.

Your wife a local girl?

Aye, oh aye.

What was her name?

Janet, Janet McLeish.

Were they a Kirrie family?

Oh aye .. ye ken Willie Ogilvie that played the trumpet?

Oh aye, that had the Herald.

(Kirrie newspaper still printed today)

That was her brother – the Ogilvies & the McLeishes.

Kirriemuir Herald 28th October 1976

The first round of the Redhurst Cup was completed this week with another two matches. In the first game, Spence Yeaman, holder of the cup for the past three years, was in opposition to Stan Milne. Spence's rink of Athole Mollison, Malcolm McBeath and Jim Strathearn seemed to be in command of the situation and were leading 9-6 going into the last end. At the second last end, Stan's rink was making a bid to narrow the gap when disaster struck for sweepers John Gilmour and Quentin Grant. So great were the Doc's efforts that he broke the shaft of his broom, fell on the stone and sent Quentin crashing to the ice. Nothing daunted Stan's rink made a great fight back at the last end and took four shots to beat the holder 10-9.

Then the family came along?

Aye, aye Pat was born 45, Catherine was ten year after that 55; ten year a tween them It was funny- aye ken their age - I'm 91, this year, Pat's 61 this year and Catherine's 51.

And you're bound to have a few grandchildren as well are there?

Fower grandchildren and two great grandchildren.

So there was three o' ye and some were born in the Town Hall?

Twa o' us, Keith & Sheila wiz born in the Town Hall.

So your father & mother were they like caretakers of the Town Hall then?

Och! they were in the Town Hall for years. My father and them were in the Toon Hall when the Poles were here –that's when it was handy bein' a tailor – you got a lot of work from them – especially the officers, they had to be.. ho ho.

Now you said you served your time in the factory and then during the war you worked in the foundry in Dundee. Did you come back to work in the factory here?

Aye, you see I served my time in the Wilkies and then I came back and got a job in the Gairie. I was there until I retired.

(Gairie – Ogilvy Bros textile works)

And so your job was as an engineer, so were you repairing, maintaining the machines?

Aye.

Ave got a question here about the bummers.
(A very loud steam operated deep sounding whistle)

Well, wiz funny, we wiz just speaking about that on Sunday whan Catherine and them… I aye thocht that the bummers stopped when the war started but no.

Aye when I was a laddie the bummers were going. It was in the 60's.. I'll tell you whan they stopped. It's

when the factories went all electric.. that's whan it wiz. When that was I couldna' tell you, I was in the factory at that time of course.

So what was your first bummer then, what time of the day?

Half past five in the morning, that was to get you up.

So that was really like an alarm clock?

Aye aye ha ha.

So did you hear it a ower Kirrie did you?

Oh God aye an' then at five to six syne..

And that was…

Tae gie ye five minutes to get in.

And was there a bummer at lunchtime?

Then there was a bummer at ten o'clock. You worked from six to nine, ten till one an two to five… an six to nine on a Saturday.

And did ye ging hame between….?

Oh aye ye went hame.

So six till nine, ten till one and two to five so there would have been three bummers that went.

Let's just say up until you were 25 years old, what sort of interests did you have during the winter, the summer, weekends – dancing, the pictures?

Oh aye we used tae go to the pictures - oh aye that would be a weekly occasion. In the winter time we used to go away oot to the country dancing – used tae go to Cortachy and Memus and a' place.

On your bike?

No no there was twa or three o' us in a car…. We were after twa lasses there ye see.

Lets go back to the curling – so you're up at the Glengate rink, you're playing off a crampet – you just had the two rinks so you'd had at least 4 crampets?

(crampet – a heavy studded metal plate on which the curler placed both feet, forerunner to the hack used today)

That's right aye.

Would they have been made locally?

I've nae idea, they were there when I started.

Aye they could have been there a long time. And you were telling me that it was just enough to cover a coin that you sprayed on the rink. So how did you get the crampet attached to the ice? Did you just chap it doon?

Aye, as I mind right they had spikes in them.

Aye, I've seen the crampet when it was at a loch. And did you have proper curling brushes?

Oh yes aye, they were a' in the hut and a'thing.

And you were telling me that you and the other guy from the factory used to ging up to prepare the rink.

And you sprayed it and left it for about an hour or so and if it happened to snaw then did you have scrapers?

Oh aye you hud tae gae up and clear it.

Did you have special scrapers for that?

No, no that I can mind of.

Just shovels and things?

Aye.

What aboot marking out the rink then – that be your job? How did you do your circles?

They were a marked there you see and they were showin' through the ice.

Oh, they were painted on?

Aye they were painted on.

So just the same as indoor. So was there a barrier at each end to stop the stones?

Oh aye, just a wee ledge.

'Cos I remember somebody saying that stones that had been used up there got awfa rough.

Aye they wid be kinda rough I suppose.

Were they ever polished?

No that I ken of.

Did you ever turn them on to the other side?

No that I ken o'.

You see we used tae dae that up at Cortachy – sometimes – you usually needed the very fast side but I remember being up at one time – I've got a set of stones which had obviously been looked after and we were up at Cortachy or Glen Queich and the ice was so good I had to put mine on to the rougher side.

You said to me that you played Cortachy for the Durston Trophy?

Aye, that's whan it started.

Aye and that would be sometimes up the Glengate and sometimes at Cortachy?

Aye. It was year aboot and if Cortachy wisna' fit to play they just cam doon to us.

When you went up to Cortachy would you lads have taken your own stones up?

Oh aye you took your stones up-

You'll have another wee tottie in there?

Aye

(sound of the crater going into the glass)

Going back to the curling competitions, did you play Points at the Glengate?

Oh aye, no I dinna think we ever did that.

They must have been played in the past certainly but….

No there was never onything like that. There was never onything serious- the only eens that were serious wiz the Redhurst Cup.   *(Knock-out competition)*

Tell me who gave the Redhurst Cup, was it the dairyman? ..do you remember who gave the Redhurst Cup?

A'll tell you what I think, I might be wrang mind but wha I think gie the Redhurst Cup was Chae Ogilvy.

Did he stay at Redhurst?   *(House name on Brechin Road)*

Aye he stayed at Redhurst, I'm mair sare o that … mind he had the joiners business in Kirrie.

That's why it would have been called the Redhurst Cup.

Am mair sare that is 'cos we has een alang at the bowling green the very same and I think he gave one to the curlers and one to the bowlin'.

I don't know why I thought it was a dairyman that was involved with that.

Oh that was fut dae ye ca him oot at ………..

Tannadice?   *(Village on way to Brechin)*

Tannadice- Stewart.

Oh a'll tell you what J.C.Stewart against Farfar.

(Annual 3-rink match against Forfar Curling Club)

Ha ha ha.

Oh that's a guid competition an' that must have been started aboot your time?

Oh aye it was started.

Early 50's maybe? I hope you beat Farfar a lot of times.

Ha ha ha oh Christ that's right J.C.Stewart.

So he was the dairyman at?

Aye at Tannadice.

We dinna often beat Forfar nowadays but there was a couple of times when Forfar had their Curlers' Court the night before and then we beat them the next day.

(hangovers)

Ha ha.

You were President of the club 1961 to 62 and 1962 to 63.

That's right, aye.

Did you have a dance at that time? Curlers dance?

No…no …no that I mind o'.

Right, tell me about Curlers Courts.

(Initiation of new curlers into the Brotherhood)

Oh Christ, ha ha some toppers ah tell you.

Where did you hold them- in the Airlie? Or the Ogilvy maybe?

(Both local hotels)

Well, year aboot. I'll tell you whan I was made.. mind ye Mackie at Benshie? Brought me up in his shoulders and tilt me doon, ha ha aye that's true.

(Lord Mackie of Benshie – farmer & Liberal Peer)

It hasna' changed much.

No it hasna' changed much at a'.

'Am aye quite glad to hear that because if you go to some o' the newer clubs it's just .. there's no tradition; it's just a lot of horseplay nowadays. They've actually lost that but we've always tried tae keep it in Kirrie according to what's been done in the past – we never really embarrass people and we never have people really upset.

No yer richt enough.

Well ah, ah remember Jim Moffat, ach a wisna in the curlin' club a' that lang, maybe a few years and he said there's an invite tae the Cortachy Curling Club, they're having a Curlers Court – would you maybe go and represent Kirrie. I didna' ken what curlers courts was of course and off I went like a lamb to slaughter – 'course I was made.

(Jim Moffat, Banker & Club Secretary)

Aye! But I was there.

Were you there!?

I made ya. Do you no mind o' that?

Aye there was a big crowd and I'll tell you who was in the chair- David Wardhaugh. *(Estate Factor)*

Now we've covered the courts; ye'd have been My Lord and My Lord's Officer tae?

Aye.

And the other thing that has, was, a noticeable change and it just seemed to come in almost overnight- when you used to go to the curlin' you went off with your partner for a dram.

Aye, that's right.

Twice during the game?

Aye.

I seem to remember goin' off wi' Dave Ewart – he was a skip when I started *(Livestock auctioneer)*

And ah had.. a great liking for him – ach he took to me as well because he used tae come round every Hogmanay – never missed a trick and Iain Ewart as well.

I quite believe that.

Aye and I'd played this stone right tae the button, just exactly as he'd asked me to and am fair chuffed ya see, gaen up the ice and he says "McKiddie! - two and a half turns is all you're allowed tae come up here – that thing went aboot five turns." Ya ken Dave Ewart and I'd maybe been playing second I suppose and it came to a measure you see, and I wandered up to sort of say that one's definitely lying and he says .. "McKiddie …F--- off"

I kent he would say that ha ha. Onything else noo? 'Cos this is braw I dinna ken if you're enjoying it.

I'm thoroughly enjoying it…

I'm some glad I took up the curlin' onyway….Sometimes I sit doon an' think o' a' the memories I have wi' curlin' 'cos tae be quite honest wi' you, it was one o' my best times when I was curlin'.

Another wee nightcap?

Ach aye, aye.

I'm sure you'll no' be any the worse in the morning.

(Lovely sound of drink being poured into two glasses)

Wallace, thank you for agreeing to do this interview, which I've found extremely interesting and I think we've both enjoyed it. When Kirriemuir Curling Club celebrates its bicentenary in 2009 it is our intention to have printed a commemorative history of the club. Hopefully this interview will be included, which will be a fascinating insight into curling of old to be enjoyed by the curlers of the future.

Kirriemuir Curling Club
Items from the Accounts

13th February 1873	Curling stones to Kilnhill	2/-
	Farm 2 m east of Kirrie Brechin Road	
July 1874	To Adamson – Pond rent for 1874.	5/-
18th December 1874	Wishart 'watching pond' for 1874.	10/-
May 1875	To Pub. Park – rent of pond for 1874.	5/-
15th January 1875	Paid for liquor used at making of curlers.	12/-
Feb. 1878	Paid Mr. Taylor Horsehirer for trap to match at Tannadice.	18/6
29th January 1879	Paid A. Whammond for covered Waggonette to Blairgowrie.	£1.5/-
28th March 1879	Paid Dundee Advertiser for advertising stone found.	2/-
24th June 1880	Paid James Davidson, Solicitor 2 years rent of pond to Marchimas 1879.	10/-
31st January 1881	Paid Thomas Lawson, Sandyford in repayment of railway fares of Curlers at Stanley on occasion of match with Logiealmond club.	£2. 9/-
January 1881	By cash from Thomas Lawson, Sandyford – Proceeds of Stoup at Dinner.	13/-

Kirriemuir Herald - 23rd February 1978
Outdoor play at Cortachy

Cortachy and Kirriemuir clubs took advantage of the continuing hard frost to play their Durston Trophy game outdoors on the pond at Cortachy.

The trophy was originally donated for that purpose but in recent years most of the matches have had to be held indoors. Kirrie, holder for the past three years had Jim Smith(skip) with Bruce Paul and Stan Milne and John Buttar, both experiencing outside curling for the first time. The second Kirrie rink was Ian Ewart (skip), Lindsay Brown, Dudley Dorman and Jim Moffat.

At the half way stage Kirrie looked to be well on the way to retaining the trophy with Jim Smith leading 9-3 against John Stewart(skip), Hugh Hood, Ray Caird and Will Gibson. The other Cortachy rink of W. Bain, Cy Mitchell, Chic Morris and Bert Sutherland were holding their own and drawing five all.

It was about this stage of the game that Dudley Dorman and Lindsay Brown seemed to be unsure whether they were playing for Kirrie or Cortachy and removed Jim Moffat's stones with unfailing regularity to the delight of the spectators. It was the last end before Ian Ewart got another shot but too late to affect the result and his rink went down 11-6.

Meantime Cortachy had been whittling away Jim Smith's lead and going into the last end were down 11 shots to 9. This meant that Smith required to get a four to retain the trophy for Kirrie. With encouraging cries of "Jim'll fix it" from the sidelines the Kirrie rink lay three shots with just the skips to play.

A rocket from Jim removed a Cortachy stone but in the process removed some of the Kirrie stones. The result was that Jim could only salvage a single shot to make the score 12-9.

Overall Cortachy triumphed by 20 shots to 18 to regain the cup. The cup was filled with the remains of the 'refreshments' required by the teams to keep warm and toasts drunk to the victors.

Photo Gallery

BELOW:
A family success story as Nicholas Dorman (aged 18) drawn with his father, Dudley, won the KCC Annual Pairs Competition in 1983.

ABOVE:
KIRRIEMUIR CURLING CLUB
TROPHY WINNERS 1977-78
J. Strathearn S. Upton C. McKiddie
J. Moffat A. Bruce B. Mollison I. Ewart

BELOW:
The handsome solid silver Points Cup showing curling scenes presented to Kirrie Curling Club by Sir Thomas Munro, Bart, Lindertis in 1865.

ABOVE:
At Forfar Indoor Sports, 2009, President Cameron McKiddie (2nd from rt) presents from Lt. Runner-up Points – Ian Cran, Points Cup – Ewan Cameron, Handicap Points - Paul McLaren.

Kirrie Curler Ian Melrose at Forfar Indoor Sports 2009

'Celebrating an 'eight ender' in style'
Highland International Week of Curling
Aviemore Ice Rink 1997
Jim Strathearn, Helen Morrison
Pat Strathearn, Cameron McKiddie

ROTARY INTERNATIONAL CURLERS

Colin Smith	Canada Tour 1992
Cameron McKiddie	Canada Tour 1984
Jim Strathearn	Canada Tour 1988
Roy Davidsosn	Canada Tour 1996

Every four years, a team of 22 Rotary Curlers from Scotland have a 3-4 week Tour of Canada and in the intervening period a team of Rotary Curlers from Canada tour Scotland.

KCC President presents Redhurst Cup to
Gordon Thomson 2009

Kirrie Curlers in action at Forfar Indoor Sports 2009

Curling by Electricity

A' curlers keen in days gone by,
As nicht came on their stanes laid by
And besoms could nae langer ply,
They hadna Electricity.

They rather liked to meet with friends
O'er toddy and guid beef and greens,
In truth, they didna care twa preens
The want o' Electricity.

But if they ever curled at nicht,
They had to play by candle-licht,
And oh! It was a dreary sicht,
For want o' Electricity.

For then they couldna even see
What stanes were lying near the tee,
A spunk then gied them licht a wee,
In place o' Electricity.

Lichted by its effulgent ray
The rink is now as bright as day,
A' through the nicht we noo can play
Wi' help o' Electricity.

We see the rink from end to end,
Ken wi' what force the stanes to send,
And to which side the bias tend,
An' a' by Electricity.

The skip could never see till now
The pace the stanes came up the 'howe*,'
Or when his men should ply the 'cowe*,'
For want o' Electricity.

But noo we can the besom ply,
And 'soop, men, soop' is heard the cry,
'He's o'er the "hogg" – noo let him die,'
An' a' by Electricity.

*howe – hollow * cowe - broom*

But time and tide nae man can stop,
St. Stephen's chimes oot twal o'clock,
We think its noo high time to stop
Oor game by Electricity.

Noo 'elbow out' or ' elbow in'
Is heard aboon the shouts and din,
Or maybe 'wick and curl in'
By help o' Electricity.

All honour be to King and Brown,
Nae king sae weel deserves a crown,
We'll mak' it o' the bonnie broom,
They've gien us Electricity.

A.G. (Edinburgh Northern Club.)

A CLERICAL CURLER

During a spell of frost an old minister, before dismissing his congregation one Sunday, remarked: 'My brethren, there's nae mair hairm speakin' it oot than thinkin' it in. Gin the frost hauds I intend to be on the ice at nine o'clock the morn's mornin'.'

R.C.C.C. Annual 1931-32

**Original painting by Gill Urquhart, wife of KCC Secretary,
Dave, which she sent as Christmas cards 2008**

Kirriemuir Herald 24th January 1980

Members were deeply shocked at the sudden death last week of Jim Moffat who for 12 years as Secretary/Treasurer gave dedicated service to the club and it was largely through his endeavour and enthusiasm that the club is now at its present strength. He will be sadly missed by all.

In the annual battle against Cortachy for the Durston trophy, conditions on Saturday were perfect for the match to be played outdoors. Kirrie's rinks were Drummond Herd(skip), J.Strathearn, L. Brown and B. Mollison and Dave Torrie(skip), B.Paul, D. Dorman and M.McVittie. The Kirrie team though well fortified in spirit took a little time to get used to outside ice and to cope with the rigours of the day after a Round Table Burns Supper, losing a total of 7 shots at the first ends. Dave Torrie's team however fought back to win 9-4 but Drummonds team, rarely in the hunt went down four shots to 12 giving Cortachy overall victory after a most enjoyable afternoon's curling.

Kirriemuir Herald 4th December 1980

Thursday saw the first annual competition between Kirrie and Aberlemno for the Ed Weighton trophy presented by Mrs Weighton in memory of her late husband's long association with the clubs of Kirrie and Aberlemno. In three enjoyable and keenly fought games it was rather appropriate that the trophy was won by Mrs Weighton's son in law, Jim Smith who skipped his team to a 11-8 victory. It was also a clean sweep to Kirrie, Cameron McKiddie winning his game by two shots and Lindsay Brown grabbing one shot with a perfectly played final stone of his match.

'Wick An' Curl In.'

A SONG FOR CURLERS

Whan luck's again' ye, an' the hoose
Is blockit up wi' stanes,
An' yer opponents , awfu' crouse*,
Are countin' up their gains;
There's aye a shot, a bonny shot,
A shot that's sure to win –
To draw up till an orra* stone,
An' wick an' curl in.

An' sae ye'll find it a' thro' life:
Whan failure nips yer pride,
An' disappointment's cruickit form
Comes hirplin' whare ye bide:
There's aye a way to Fortune's smiles,
An' takin't is nae sin,
A bonny shot for mense an' skill –
To wick an' curl in.

Yon jidge that wags his curly pow
Sae sagely ower a plea,
Yin better stocked wi' law and lair
Ye'd think there couldna be;
But losh! He's jist been wide awake
Whan ither folk were blin',
An' never let a chance gang by
To wick and curl in.

Then, brithers, let us bide oor time,
An' cautious let us play
Each ticklish shot in life's big game,
That's hoo to win the day.
Dame Fortune irate shows her claws
To drivers doon the rin,
But smiles on him who quietly draws
A wick and curl in.

Foulden Club   *John Reid, M.A. Chaplain*

* crouse – pleased with themselves * orra – odd

Kirriemuir Herald
17th December 1981

Keen frost produced excellent playing conditions at Horniehaugh
and allowed the Glasswell Cup to be played outdoors in a two-rink
match against Cortachy. Kirrie though holders of the cup from
last year's indoor game, have rarely managed to match Cortachy at
the outdoor game. However this year in a fine match of friendly
spirited curling, Kirrie won both games, Drummond Herd's rink of
L. Brown, I. Grubb And R. Davidson having the highest win of 12-5
while Cameron McKiddie's team of J. Gilmour, M.McVittie and F.
McKenzie won 8-5.
Frost prevailed to allow one game in the Jim Moffat Memorial
Bonspiel, a new three rink outdoor competition. Dudley Dorman
with J. Strathearn, C. Dailly and J. Stuart was matched with
Cameron McKiddie's team of M.McVittie, E. Cameron and D. Forsyth.
Mastering the crampet caused early difficulties to the exponents
of the sliding delivery and for six ends it was neck and neck at
3-3. However with great support from Mike McVittie, Cameron won
the last four ends to give him a handsome 13-3 victory and must be
fancied to gain the trophy. Hopefully, Jack Frost allowing, the
remaining games will be played the next few days.
If revenge is sweet, then Roy Davidson must have a very sweet
tooth, turning Drummond Herd a whiter shade of pale when he
crushingly defeated the League leaders 18 shots to 0. With a grand
display of accurate leading from Tom Steele, ably backed by E.
Cameron, and B. Paul, Roy played a mastery tactical game giving no
quarter to Drummonds rink of D. Dorman, A. Mollison and M.McBeath.

The Music o' the Year is Hush'd,

The music o' the year is hush'd,
In bonny glen and shaw, man;
And winter spreads o'er nature dead,
A winding-sheet o' snaw, man.
O'er burn and loch the warlock frost,
A crystal brig has laid, man;
The wild -geese screaming wi' surprise,
The ice-bound wave ha'e fled, man.

Up, Curler! Frae your bed so warm,
And leave your coaxing wife, man;
Gae get your besom, tramps, and stane,
And join the friendly strife, man;-

For on the water's face are met,
Wi' mony a merry joke, man,
The tenant and his jolly laird,
The pastor and his flock, man.

The rink is swept – the tees are mark'd –
The bonspiel is begun, man;-
The ice is true – the stanes are keen -
Huzza! for glorious fun, man!
The skips are standing at the tee,
To guide the eager game, man;
Hush! not a word:- but mark the broom,
And tak' a steady aim, man.

Here draw a shot; - there lay a guard;-
And here beside him lie, man;-
Now let me feel a gameser's hand;-
Now in this bosom die, man.
There fill the port, and block the ice;
We sit upon the tee, man !
Now tak' this in-ring sharp and neat,
And mak' their winner flee, man.

How stands the game? It's eight and eight!
Now for the winning shot, man!
Draw slow and sure, and tak' your aim -
I'll sweep you to the spot, man!
The stane is thrown, - it glides alang,
The besoms ply it in, man;-
Wi' twisting back the player stands,
And eager breathless grin, man.

A moment's silence still as death,
Pervades the anxious thrang, man;
Then sudden bursts the victor's shout,
Wi' hollas loud and lang, man.

Triumphant besoms wave in air,
And friendly banters fly, man;
Whilst, cold and hungry, to the inn
Wi' eager steps they hie, man.

Now fill ae bumper – fill but ane -
And drink wi' social glee, man
May curlers on life's slippery rink,
Frae cruel rubs be free, man.
Or should a treacherous bias lead,
Their erring course ajee, man,
Some friendly in-ring may they meet
To guide them to the tee, man.

HENDRY DUNCAN
R.C.C.C.Annual 1938-39

Kirriemuir Herald 11th February 1982

In the J.C.Stewart trophy against the 'auld enemy' Forfar Curling club, Kirrie reached a new low when Forfar trounced them 51 shots to 17. the only team on form was John Gilmour's rink of J. Smith, M. McBeath and A. Bruce who lead 9-1 after 5 ends but lost the remaining ends and the match 9-13.

Stan Milne's rink of I. Fraser, J. Strathearn and A. Bell didn't score until the 7th end to trail 1-11 losing finally 4-15. However it was Cameron McKiddie with his team of B.Leslie, J.Stuart and R.Brown who had the misfortune to be on the receiving end of Ray Caird's rink *(Pharmacist)*, Ray dispensing bitter medicine as he galloped to a 23-4 win. Coaching classes are to be instigated immediately.

The Grand Match

Painting by Joyce Grubb of the last Grand Match held at
Lake of Mentieth on 7th February 1979

The Grand Match is an outdoor curling bonspiel in which the North of Scotland plays against the South, the dividing line being decided by officials of the Royal Caledonian Curling Club.

However before such a match can be contemplated, it requires a prolonged period of very low temperatures to form ice thick enough for the purpose, and will only start to be considered when the depth of ice measures at least 5 inches. Global warming whether cyclical or man made or a bit of both has made this spectacular event increasingly rare.

Since the first Grand match held at Penicuik in 1847

there have only been a total of 33 matches played, all but eight played at Carsebreck, other venues being Linlithgow(photo page 8), Lochwinnoch, Loch Leven and Lake of Mentieth.

The smallest number of rinks, 24 was at the first match at Penicuik while the match at Carsebreck in 1935 involved a record of 644 rinks. As a matter of record the South has had 25 wins to the North's 8.

The average frequency of matches from 1847 to 1912 was every 2.44 years while from 1912 to the present day the frequency has dropped to 16 much to the frustration of our keen curlers.

Kirriemuir Herald 26th September 1985

Henry Havenga showed great promise in his first ever game, finding his weight and direction early; his only fall from grace being a "burnt" stone when his double salchow was not quite up to Torvill and Dean standard!

It is now thirty years since curlers were able to come from a' the airts to partake in the Grand Match held at Lake of Mentieth on 7th February 1979 so the outlook is bleak.

However, excitement grew in 2002 when a prolonged cold spell produced 5 inches of ice at Piper Dam between Dundee and Perth. Urgent messages were dispatched to clubs to get ready, causing a flurry of activity as curling stones were set outside to cool, crampits, long forgotten, unearthed and those lucky curlers selected to play prepared for a day of excitement.

However 'Jack Frost' once again departed, a thaw set in and curlers' hopes were dashed once again.

Future chances of the Grand Match being held?

Speaking to the RCCC Grand Match convenor, Jim Paterson of the Kinross Club in July this year (2009), he was of the opinion that with milder winters there was little likelihood of the Match being played in the foreseeable future. Not withstanding the lack of severe winters, he considered that in this day and age of public liability and health and safety, that previous venues would be considered unsafe to stage such a large event. Piper Dam would be the likely choice as the water is not very deep and the area is easily accessible. Jim continues to hold instructional sessions for the marking of the ice – a huge task in itself and planning and policing guidelines have been established. What a marvellous spectacle it would be at Piper Dam, not only for the thousands of curlers and spectators alike but particularly for the owners of the upmarket properties overlooking the dam. So curlers must hope that John Frost returns, sufficiently long and

Grand Match 1979

strong, so that the roar of the stone can again echo over the ice, to be matched by the roar of excited curlers as they can once again enjoy this rare event.

It is certainly possible, that in some parts of Scotland, outdoor curling could still be enjoyed on small shallow ponds or even more likely on artificial outdoor concrete pads which, with just sufficient frost and a light spraying of water the game can be played. In 1980 my own club, Kirriemuir refurbished their artificial two rink pad in preparation for a hard winter which sadly did not occur and the location has since been lost to housing development.

Kirriemuir Herald 10th November 1983
Certain members should note that to protect the ice surface the "no smoking" rule has been extended to exclude the taking of snuff while curling.

The late Alan Bruce who liked a little snuff during the game dropped the whole tin on the ice, the evidence remaining for several weeks. At an infamous AGM, most attending sampled Alan's snuff, the resulting sneezing totally disrupting the rest of the evening.

Sent by Dr Sidey to the Manager of the Royal Pond at Carsebreck (R. Taylor) on the eve of a Grand Match.

When winter nichts are lang and cauld,
And snaw is happin house and hauld,
My certy but the man is bauld
Wha says that toddy
Will ere do harm to young and auld,
To soul or body.

I rede ye on the drink we send,
The best – an auld and famous blend,
There's no' a headache though ye spend
It a' on toddy;
And it will care and caukers rend
Frae soul and body.

Sae, my dear sir, e'en take your dram,
'Twill serve your anxious thought to calm;
Whenever the big match makes you qualm
Jist take your toddy.
And syne ye needna care a --------
For ony body.

RCCC Annual 1890-91

Kirriemuir Herald
28th February 1985

There was no shortage of volunteers for the outdoor match against Cortachy played in almost perfect conditions. In the first match Drummond Herd, Jim Strathearn, Mike McVittie and Brian Mollison showed great mastery of the outdoor game to put Kirrie on the way to victory. However in the second match started somewhat later, Kirrie was struggling and despite some spirited play from Cameron McKiddie, Dudley Dorman, Dave Torrie and Gordon Ager, they could do little to stem the tide as Cortachy swept to a 11 shot advantage after 8 ends. Responding to threats and encouragement from Drummond's rink, Cameron's team scrambled singles to tie the overall match and in an extra deciding end Kirrie picked up one shot to retain the Glasswell Cup.

Kirriemuir Herald
24th October 1985

Carolyn Strathearn(sub), a promising young curler with a style and grace quite unlike her father helped complete Iain Grubb's rink of Bruce Paul, and Tom Morris in their match against Cameron McKiddie, Derek Shearer, Ian Nicol and Mike Wilson. In a closely fought game, Iain came from behind to score 5 at the last end to win 12-8.

Kirriemuir Herald 13th February 1986

In the other semi(Redhurst), Jack Donaldson and his rink of Tom Morris, Bill Keillor and Neil Rae were struggling to keep up with the heavy handed tactics of Jim Strathearn and his rink of Chris Dailly, Gordon Ager and Drummond Herd, Jack taking singles at three ends while Jim scored a four, a three and a one to be comfortably ahead 8-3 with four ends to play. Jack crept closer with singles at six, seven, eight and nine and in a classic last end Jim kept the house clear. With a hitch to the specs, Jack played his last stone for a split to lie two. All was quiet as Jim let go a rocket to remove one for the match and when last seen his stone was still thundering towards Kirriemuir having missed its mark, giving Jack and his delighted team a finals place on ends won.

In the Points Competition Cameron McKiddie took an early lead, which he maintained to win with 39 points, a record score in the Points 120 year history.

The Grand Match at Carsebreck

Two days after submitting, what I thought was my final draft, of 'Celebrating Curling – The Roarin' Game' to the Publishers, serendipity led me to this captivating account of 'The Grand Match at Carsebreck', which my earlier research had missed.

I make no apology for including this account in its entirety in this compilation. Furthermore I have deliberately avoided inserting photos or sketches among the original text so that the reader can conjure up their own colourful images of the excitement of this historic event. This is painting by pen of the highest degree which, I think even Carlyle himself (see text) would have acclaimed. I am thrilled to have the opportunity to bring this outstanding, graphic account once more into print. Ed.

An account of the Grand Match of the Royal Caledonian Curling Club can no more be left out of a Jubilee Book in honour of its foundation in Scotland than the Coronation Day of Her Most Gracious Majesty, Queen Victoria – whose name of Royalty it bears – could be left out of any Jubilee Book in honour of her accession to the throne of Great Britain and Ireland. The one is in commemoration of the Union of many scattered "Branches" in one glorious Sovereign; the other is in commemoration of the Union of many scattered Clubs in one "Grand Club". The one has gone on increasing her dominions, during these fifty years, until she has become the Empress of a world upon which the sun never sets; the other has gone on increasing its dominions, during these past fifty years, until it has become the Emperor of the world of Curling, upon which also it may be said the sun never sets. And although, in the eyes of the world, the one is not to be compared in the same breath as the other, yet in the eyes of every "keen, keen curler," the one is not thought unworthy, any more than the other, to have a Jubilee Celebration in memory of its origin, and medals struck and a Book written in commemoration of that event. Thus as the tamer associations of Accession day are to the joy and rejoicing of the Queen's Birthday, so are the tamer duties of the General Meeting of the Royal Caledonian Curling Club to the joy and rejoicing over the Grand Match at Carsebreck.

At this General Meeting of Representative members, the preliminaries for the Grand Match are arranged— the places appointed, generally Carsebreck; and the time named, generally winter, weather permitting and ice holding. The Committee of this Meeting then sends out, through its worthy Secretary, circulars to all the affiliated Clubs throughout the kingdom, inviting them to send a number of rinks to the great contest. It is between the North and the South of the Island, or what have been in former times between the Saxon and the Gael. Returns are made; the draw takes place; and the "correct card" is issued. It is not, however, to any Race Meeting, or like thing of the kind, but only to a friendly match at curling. There is no betting or laying on of bets; no losing or gaining of money, but the losing or gaining of a little honour; no Welsher's or suicide's grave, but brotherly fairness and rivalry. There may be a little "scratching" the day before, but there is no "hedging" – every one must come to the "scratch," and do his duty. It may be called the Derby Day of Scotland. The Parliament House with its "Lords and Lawyers" does not indeed adjourn over this day, as the Imperial Parliament with its "Lords and Commons" adjourns over the Derby Day; but every other match or meeting, whether at "market, kirk or fair," is "off" on that day. It is said that Carlyle was once offered £1000 by one of the London newspapers to write an account of the Derby. He refused. But from what we know of him as a word-painter of scenes and scenery we can conceive what a glorious word picture he would have drawn of it! How he would have begun with a description of the trial and the training, betting and bargaining, waiting and watching of a year. How would he have described the eve of the Derby in club-room and tap-room, in house and in hall, in hut and den, with all their roar and uproar; and its preparation of hampers of champagne and ginger-pop, and boxes of sandwiches and sweetmeats with a slight sensation of the crater, or a nip of the Auld Kirk. How would he have portrayed the "road" and "rail" to Epsom; the one with its crowds of equestrians and pedestrians, its carriages and wheelbarrows, its carts and coster-mongereries, amid a whirlwind of dust and dirt; the other with its jostling crowds of men and women, of all shapes and sizes, colours and hues, old and young, crammed into the carriages like herrings in a barrel, yet "laughing and daffing" as if making merry were the one object of life. How he would have drawn "over the downs so free" – the wind playing with the rags of the beggar as well as with the flutterings of some gay human butterfly in the shape of the "girl or masher of the period;" the pinched and hungry look of some, and the swollen out and debauched look of others; the swilling of ale and beer, brandy and soda in this place, and the gormandising on bread and beef, pies and porter in that; the courting and cooing in this corner, and the fencing and fighting in that; the preaching and praying here, and the cursing and swearing there; the buying and selling of some, and the cheating and swindling of others – all waiting in expectation and preparing for the great Race. How he would have described the paddock with its jostling and noise, its betting and "barring;" the grand stand with its tiers of beauty, wealth and nobility; and the general concourse of spectators of every people, nation, language and tongue. And then how he would have pictured out the "saddling" and "walk past;" "the fall of the flag," and the cry *they are off*; the craning of necks and the scope of the field glass; the "turning of Tottenham Corner," and "the straight run home;" – the whole ending with a confusion worst confounded than that of the confusion of tongues at the Tower of Babel.

It would require the pen of a Carlyle to give an account of all this; and it would require no less a pen to give an account of the Grand Match at Carsebreck. It may be a humbler theme, but there are the same sort of good things to be described without almost any of the bad. There is the same sort of hope and expectancy throughout the year. There is no certainty, and there is no betting. The same kind of preparation is made on the eve of the Grand Match. The weather prophets are consulted throughout the land; the barometers are tapped with a thousand fingers; the moon and stars are looked at with ten thousand eyes, whether she is upright and clear, or on her back, and surrounded with a halo; and whether there are twinkling, or steady in a blue sky. There are many wet rags hung out of the windows as would delight the eyes of the raggatherers, and as many cups and saucers with water set out as would tea the whole poor of the land.

It has been ringing frost for a few days, but Cassels or Smith may be deceived, as they have often been deceived. The flasks, however, are filled, the sandwiches made, the change of socks for the gudeman got ready, and the rugs, mits, and comforters prepared. There has been the usual examination of handles and stones, of brooms and besoms, of crampets and tees; and now all things are ready for the start. Then the old curler, having drunk his last tumbler for the night with success to the match, puts on literally and metaphorically his night-cap, and retires to rest, but not to sleep –only at times, after having examined his natural and artificial weatherglasses, to dream of frost and snow, hail and ice, "hogs and draws," "guards and lies," "inwicks" and "outwicks," "ports" and "shots." There is little rest for the gudewife for that "ae nicht," They are all up betimes. The knights of the "broom," who are to do battle at Carsebreck today, have thrown off dull sleep, and have joyfully "risen to the occasion." From Maiden's Head to John o' Groats, and from the East Neuk of Fife to the Point of Ardnamurchan, there is a hurry and a haste as on the eve of Waterloo. There is the running to and fro, and the cart "rattling o'er the stony street." There is the "mounting in hot haste the steed, the mustering squadron," and the clattering car, pouring forward with impetuous speed. There is the "Cameron's Gathering" and the *Curling* "Note of Lochiel," Evan's cry and Donald's summons, and all hurrying by road and rail over hill and valley stream and plain, and by woodland and brake, towards the great rendezvous of the day – Carsebreck. But where is Carsebreck?-- you may ask that of the Marines. You might as well ask, Where is "the Man in the Moon"? It is "at the back o' beyont." And yet many a village urchin will tell you it is where his " father gangs tae curl." They say it is near some Greenloanin' in the Highlands. We issue forth then with "John," "Ben," and "Wullie" – rare fellows, from "under" the morning shade of the Ochils, and find ourselves soon with the iron horse at Stirling. Here they are already all in a bustle. The platform is covered with curling-stones of every size and colour, from the dark speckled Crawford-John to the light spotted Ailsa Craig, and the ebony black Tarth Water.

It is a keen crisp morning. The icicles are hanging from the eaves. It is a day to delight the hearts of curlers. It is very unlike others we have experienced here, when the water was running from the roofs as from a spout, and when we anticipated and after experienced a loch covered with slush to our ankles, and when the stones were "swimming" through the water, and "Ben's" new boots would never squeak more.

We have just "one small one" to keep our courage up. There is to be no more at present. It is dangerous in the morning. It puts the shakers on, if it does not put them off. But the trains are arriving from the south, east and west. They are "bung-fu' o' men." Some are singing, others shouting, some are reading the newspapers, others are playing at Ha'penny Nap or a Penny a Point, and Sixpence the Rubber. They hail us with "Mac" from the open windows, and we elbow our way in to one of the least thronged carriages. Here they are from the lands of the Bold Buccleuch of the Border, the Douglas's and Johnstones of Annandale and Nithsdale, and from the faraway-off wilds of Galloway. There they are from "Auld Reekie," the Lothians and the Kingdom of Fife, and from the Land of Burns, the Wards of Lanarkshire, and Glasgow and Greenock. They will sing you almost *in personae* " Braw braw Lads of Gala Water," "Ye Banks and Braes of Bonnie Doon," "Loudoun's Bonnie Woods and Braes," "Afton Water," or "The Boatie Rows."

We are again, however, on the "move" to meet the men of the North. They are now on the like "move" from Perth. They come to do battle against the Sassenach, but not as of yore with broad sword and braid claymore, but with the broom and the "channel stane." How altered the circumstances, and may we not give the palm to curling! Can we not sing, with a little alteration, of one name:-

> **"Cam ye by Athol, lad w' the philabeg,**
> **Down by the Tummel or Banks of the Garry,**
> **Saw ye the lads in their bonnets an' white cockcades**
> **Leaving their mountains to follow Prince Charlie?"**

> **"Wha wadna join our noble chief**
> **The Drummond and Glengarry,**
> **Macgregor, Murray, Rollo, Keith,**
> **Panmure, and gallant Harry."**

> **"Macdonald's men, Clanranald's men,**
> **Mackenzie's men, Macgilvray's men,**
> **Strathallan's men, the Lowland's men**
> **Of Callander and Airlie."**

All are here. Bannochburn is not far off, and we are approaching the like marshy ground. All eyes are towards the windows to get the first view of the place of the contest. The first object that meets the gaze in the otherwise uninteresting country-side is the flag of the Lion Rampant, waving on the knoll beyond. The combatants are already on the ground in their thousands; and what may be called the regular camp-followers are also there in their thousands.

We draw slowly up at the small sideway station, and distrain in the utmost wildness and confusion. What a scurry and scramble for stones, and besoms, and "prickles." They have to be conveyed over the small wooden bridge which spans the burn that floods the marshy ground beyond into a Loch. It is a rickety concern this bridge, but little did the wiseacre think when he said in crossing it in the morning, "Take care or the whole affair will be 'Doun the burn, Davie, lad', that before evening he would return home a prophet and more than a prophet. This, however, and the fences and the snow are as nothing, and less than nothing, to the "keen, keen curler." The stones are carried by some as a couple of pigs in a poke, by others as a pair of millstones round the neck. Here they are being wheeled as a pair of miniature grindstones, and there they are being pulled or pushed along as twins in a perambulator. The orthodox way, however, is to carry them as two pails of water, with the broom under the arm, or drag them along by the neck as a drake and a duck. Such a pushing and pulling, jostling, and tumbling of men and things as was never seen since the time of the entrance into Noah's ark. Hallo! here is a regular encampment of a tinker or variety- show – there are the wooden huts of the Secretary and his assistants, and there the canvas tents of the Refreshment and Committee Rooms. There are "sweetie and gingerbread stands" and "tea and coffee stalls." They are calling the "correct card" and offering "to caddy" your stones. Our skip, with the rest of them, has dived into the booking- office and returns with the number of the rink and his marking ticket. We betake our way through the well-swept and apportioned streets of rinks to No. 35. Our opponents for the day have already arrived. We introduce ourselves without ceremony to them. They scan us, and we scan them. They are a jolly set of fellows; and they may be saying, "You're another." We look well to our stones and besoms, and then comes a breathing space. We gaze upon the scene. It is grand! It is wonderful! The district around is of no account, and it is made less so with one monotonous plain of snow; but the lords and the ladies, the marquises, dukes and "a' that," the ministers and doctors, the lawyers and lairds, the merchant-men and farmers, the artisan and workman of every degree and dress, make up for the lack of natural beauty in the scene. They are dressed in every variety of costume—from the broadcloth to the hoddin' grey, from the tunic to the kilt, from knickerbockers to the knee – breeches; with hat and scull-cap, Balmoral and Glengarry, Kilmarnock and wideawake; fez and smoking-cap. Did ever such a scene present itself to the mind's eye of him who wrote on the philosophy of clothes, and who was offered £1000 to write an account of the Derby Day? What an amount of vanity and earnestness, of pride and distinction, of skill and wisdom is throbbing through the minds of those curlers clad in the Garb of the Old Gaul. But we cease to moralise on what use all this time and talent might be turned to. It is not good for man always to be at work, any more than it is not good for him to always be alone. He must have his nose sometimes lifted from the grindstone. Life is not made up of hard cash and hardware; and "all work and no play makes Jack a dull boy." Besides, these young ladies of beauty, and these gents of chivalry are gliding past us in their skates, a pleasure to see and a joy for ever in the great kaleidoscope of this world's scene. "A thousand hearts are beating happily. Soft eyes are looking love to eyes which speak again." "But hush! hark! a deep sound strikes like a rising knell!" "Arm! arm! it is! it is – the cannon's opening roar."

Is it to be war after all then? No—it is only the small cannon on the knoll summoning us to stand to our stones and brooms instead of our guns and arms. We come to attention at once, and after another shot is fired a hundred copper or silver coins are flashing in the air, and the toss being won, a hundred voices, of what we may call Skips No.1, are crying out to their *first* men, "Now, just come up here and lie within the circle or parish." "Gi'e us a pat-lid for the first." "Be upon the snuff." "I won't blame ye if ye touch the outer ring in front." It is done or not done, with sweeping or not with sweeping. Skips No. 2 then call upon their *first* men, " I wish you to lie beside this one;" or "Never mind that ane, come up and draw for yersel'" –"Man, ye're raging and roaring;' or, Cowe him up, boys, or he'll be a hog," "hie to him." "Oh, never fash yer thoumb;" "ye'll get the whitch of it by and by," "ye're in the way of promotion," "I like to begin canny" –"No fears!"

Skips No. 1 then steps in and say to their *second* men in turn. "Draw up past that one," "break an egg upon this;" or, "lay a guard upon that," "lie beside yourself," "die at the side of this one." "Canna, men," "wait on him," "watch him," "be kind to him," "soop him up," "work before him," "gie him legs – there, that'll dae," "leave him," "he's a grand one," "a perfect beauty;" or, "hout, man; ye have thrown away yer stane," "keep straight up the howe ice," "nane of your bucking game here;" or, "riding them out," "the canny game is the best," "men kittle the ice," "clear the ring," "stand to you sides," Skips No. 2 in turn, come forward, and cry out to their *second* men alternatively –"I want you to raise your own;" or, "lie at the cheek of this stane," "tee high and nothing more," "let us soop ye;" or, "the gaird serves him," "ay, never heed that," "the guard's off, "that's better now," "ye're easily pleased;" or, "ye're weel set doon," "never own him," "haud up your hands," "they won't get that one—there that'll dae," "a regular chap-and-lie;" or, 'ye have brittled in and hidden yoursel'," "a rare cunning yin," "I'll gie ye a snuff for that yet." Or again, "What do you see of this, how much of that," indicating with broom or besom. "Do you see this "inwick' or that 'outwick.'" And the answer comes down the rink, "I see it 'a', a 'half,' or a 'quarter' of it," "I see it fine." "Do you wish it strong?"—"No, come cannily down," "dinna 'fear' or 'flee' the guard," "just to my cowe," "ye're looking weel," " I like ye," "attend to him, men," "he's a braw lad," "the very thing," "ye're a great curler," "there—

that will bother them!" "take yersel by the hand.'
"Then skips No. 1 in turn take their *third* men in hand and give the word of command in some phrases as these—" O for a guard! a kingdom for a guard," "just at my hat here, "let us soop ye;" or, "draw up through this 'port' to the face of the winner," "a little of the Kilmarnock twist with 'elbow in,'" "there are a pair of breeks for you," "tak yer wull o' them," "gie this one sixty days," "pit out the winner." "Ah, but ye're a hog instead of a gaird," "soop him my cronies—oh, soop him up—soop him up," " he's a hog," "take him by the handle," "off with him," "he's of no use;" or, "ye've done it," " a' the way," " tell him his name is Walker," " Wanderin' Willie," "stand by!" "hush man, ye've cleared the ring," "what a curler!" "Hoora! hoora!! brooms up lads." Skips No. 2, nothing daunted, step into the ring and cry out to their *third* men, "Oh, never mind them," "draw up for your ain haul," " ye've got it a' to yourself," "come straight down the broad," "never fear," "we'll soop ye," "be in front of the tee;" or, "raise" or "guard your own," "promote yoursel'," "chap and guard," "snoove away down here," "cowe him, ye dogs," "brush him up," "run before him," "bring him into the fireside, or ingle, or neuk;" or "he's a collie, tak' him by the cuff of the neck," "he's set down beside the hog," whisker him;" or. "see him through," "soop him by," "he's through a' ice and the back o' beyont."

Then Skips Nos. 1 and 2 all retire to the other end to play their shots, and the Vice-Skips take their places in turn at the ice. They are cutting out all the different points of the game—"strike" or "inwick," "draw" or "guard," "chap-and-lie" "or "wick and curl-in," "raise" or "chip the winner," and "out-wick." There are "hits" and "misses," "roarers" and "ragers," "flukes" and "flounders," "twisters" and "twirlers," "brittlers" and "legs," "siders" and "shots," "gainers" and "losers."

Thus from the first "head" or "end" the game goes merrily along, with every variety of form and fortune. What a shouting and shrieking, roar and uproar, din and confusion! That of the two hours' calling, "Great is the Diana of the Ephesians," was a mere bagatelle to this three hours' calling at the game of curling. There are shrill voices and the squeaking voices; the leather- tongued and kettle- tongued; the silver toned and the trumpet-toned; the speech which is silvern and the silence which is golden. Some are crying one thing, and some another. Some are praising outwardly, others are cursing inwardly; and all are a mixture of braid Scotch, fine English and guttural Gaelic. Oh, if all this noise and sound, this speech and language could be bottled up in the phonograph, and produced at will, what a laughable concert or entertainment it would afford! We would have all the sounds of the gamut from low C to high C, from the highest tenor to the lowest bass, with major and minor keys of every note and all the sharps and flats, quavers and demi-semi quavers of the scale. We would have high and low comedy and farce, not to speak of history and tragedy.

Then, what gesturing and posturing! Here they are on their knees who are seldom on their knees. They are "hunking and howling." Here some are on their bellies—there others are on their backs. The arms are akimbo on some hips—the hands folded over the breast of others. This runs to this side screwing his arms and legs—that one makes for the other side, contorting his body and making faces. One follows his stone for a little—another stands stock still. This player plays with the sow's back—that one stands with the Grecian bend. Here he plays as if a poker were up his back—there he plays as if he were to the mode and manner bred. This one in throwing his stone from him "fells" or "kills" it, and breaks the ice—that other one puts it down on his foot, and it goes away as smoothly as on glass. This one in throwing away his stone looks first at the farther end, and then at his feet –that other looks at his feet first, and then steadily on the thing intended. Some have brooms up, others besoms down. They are all shapes and forms, from the country cowe to the masher brush. They are held in all modes and manners. Some sweep with the force of windmills, others with the mincing gait of the housemaid. Here is calmness and dignity—there is wildness and fury. There is never a hair turned on these, but the hairs of those are flying in the wind. Hats and coats are off with some—"mits" and gloves are on with others. "Did you ever see a cat catch mice with 'mits' on?" says one—

"Did ye ever see a hen scraping with spats on?" says another. Oh! What *demons* with "sheep-shank banes," and "spindle-shanks," and "nieves as nits:" and what arms and legs with haggis fed, in all positions and posturings, would be seen if the whole of the scene were photographed in a moment of time. But there is a general hush come over the game. It is luncheon time. Mouths are now at work. Bags and pockets have been ransacked, and sandwiches and whisky are now the order of the day. Take a "nip" or a glass? A "nip" if any, if you are gaining, a glass or more if you are losing. In the one case, you cannot do better—you may do worse. In the other case, you cannot do worse—you may do better.

Why are these crowds around these rinks just finishing the last end before lunch. It is the Duke of Athol with his gillies, and the Earl of Breadalbane with his gamekeepers—all dressed in Highland costume –versus, perhaps, Lord Balfour of Burleigh with his servants, and the Earl of Mar with his dependants. It is interesting. It is humbling. It is amusing. Jack is as good as his master today. The gillies can swear their minced oaths at their lordships to-day, and the gardeners can rate their masters right heartily for not playing a good shot. But who are these flitting about among the crowd with little flags flying?—It is members of the ambulance corps, or those showing where the umpires of the match are. The arrangements are complete. It says a great deal for the committee of management. But we must buckle-to again. The game goes on apace and in the even tenor of its way. There is more shouting and yelling than ever. When wine is in wut is out. When the "spirits" are down the spirits are up. The fun grows fast and furious. Those who are down would fain to be up, and those who are up would fain be done. Time is precious. There is a pushing ahead and a holding back, but all is fair in love and warfare.

There is nothing, however, but friendship and good fellowship unless you meet in with a regular "boor" or "bore," which is seldom the case on the ice. But we are just beginning to get familiar with our opponents to name them by their shortened names, to joke with them, and rail at them, to offer them a "sweety" or "a drink"—when "Hark! that heavy sound breaks in once more." It is again the cannon on the knoll summoning us this time to cease firing our shots. There is no new "end" to be begun after this. The "head" already begun must be played out. The counting cards are summed and signed, ready to be handed in by the winner: bottles and flasks are drawn, and a thousand glasses are flashing in the air, and drained to "happy to meet you, sorry to part;" though beaten today "we hope to live to win another day." Then there is a general rush or stampede, as of the morning—but this is bedlam to it—to the trains which are standing ready—the railway arrangements also being everywhere complete. You do not need to ask your friends, as you salute them by the way, whether they are "up" or "down." look at their faces will tell you that better than any words of theirs: some are dark and lowering with despair, and disgust written on every line; others are bright and beaming, with gain and success marked in every smile and laugh. Through much pushing and jostling we reach our train at last, but no sooner have we taken our seats than the cry is made, "The bridge has gone by the boards"-- it is into the burn with men, women and children, stones, brooms and crampets. There is a general scrimmage and scramble out. Some are hanging on by the planks—others are sitting on the fences. These on this side are merry with laughter—those on the other side are blank with despair. It is a sort of a small caricature of the Tiberian Bridge and the Roman Three. The obstacle is not very formidable but the position is ludicrous in the extreme. " The hewers of wood and drawers of water," however, are here. They run a cart or two into the gap. They will see you and yours over for a sixpence, or they will even carry you over on their backs for the same. The lords and ladies resign themselves to their fate, and are ferried over, if not *a la Charon-wise*, at least *a la rusticity*. Some, however, cast their stockings and shoes, and wade through water, snow and ice, rather than pay the damage. It is plucky, but it is enough to make our flesh creep. How many colds may be caught on this day, which will end in death, we cannot tell! we cease to calculate. Where but in Scotland and at curling could you get such a crowd to meet from far and near. It is the channel stane which draws them all, as the needle to the pole. All is well that ends well. Only one leg is broken—the only mishap of the day. Beyond lies the field of contest, deserted and alone, strewn not with the wounded, dead and dying, but with broken stones, brooms destroyed, and bottles emptied. We are all in our trains at last. In moving off, those going south salute those going north with a parting cheer, to meet some other day; and we hie our way home, some singing and shouting and others sorrowing and sighing, some to be greeted heartily by the gudewife, others to be scolded for their pains—all to hear next day the South is "up."

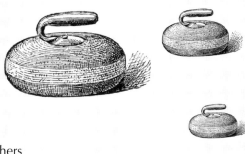

Oh! for the channel stane,

The fell gude game the channel stane!

There's no a game that e'er I saw

Can match auld Scotland's channel stane.

W. L. McD.

RCCC Annual 1890-91

Post script: While I would have liked to research who W. L. McD. was, and perhaps have included fuller details here, I must respect his choice of confining his authorship to initials alone. Ed.

The Music o' the Channel–Stane

Attend, ye curlers, young and auld,
Baith rich and puir, and a' that;
I'll sing a sang to fley the cauld,
And cheer your hearts for a' that.
For a' that and a' that,
Their gentle games and a' that;
Gi'e me the roarin' channel-stane,
The besom, tramps, and a' that.

Let foreign lads their fiddles tune,
Their pipes, guitars, and a' that;
He's but a silly feckless loon
Wha wadna laugh at a' that.
For a' that and a' that,
Their waltz, quadrille, and a' that;
'The music o' the channel-stane'
Sounds sweeter far than a' that.

The English, wi' their cricket ba's,
Their fox-huntin', and a' that,
May rend the air wi' loud huzzas,
And royal fun may ca' that.
For a' that and a' that,
Their steeple-chase, and a' that;
The chasin' o' the channel-stane
Is nobler sport than a' that.

They ca' their turtle soup sae gude,
Their fricassees, and a' that;
But beef and greens, though homelier food,
Is better far than a' that.
For a' that, and a' that,
Their cauld blamange, and a' that;
Scotch broth pits marrow in the banes,
And keeps them green for a' that.

Ours is a game for duke or lord,
Lairds, tenants, hinds , and a' that;
Our pastors, too, who preach the Word,
Whiles tak' a throw and a' that.
For a' that, and a' that,
Our different ranks, and a' that,
The chield that plays and soops the best
Is greatest man for a' that.

Then let us praise our blessed land,
Our Queen, our laws, and a' that;
May curlers, though a boisterous band,
Be loyal, true, and a' that.
For a' that, and a' that!
May curlin' thrive for a' that !
The Besom, Tramps, and Channel-stane
Is King o' games for a' that !

RCCC Annual 1888-89

Kirriemuir Herald 18th March 1982

Curlers triumph A team of curlers from the Rotary Club of Kirriemuir brought distinction to their club when they won the District final of the Scottish Rotary Ramshead Trophy held in Perth last Thursday. The rink comprising Roy Davidson (skip), Cameron McKiddie, Jim Strathearn and Ron Brown won through to the final after a close exciting semi final against Inverness, the final score being 8-5. In the final they met the holders of the trophy, Perth who knocked out Kirrie in the second round last year so it was just revenge for Roy to lead his team expertly to a well deserved 11-7 victory. The team go on to the Scottish semi final and final to be played at Hamilton Ice Rink in April when they'll be hoping that the 'Ramshead' not only returns to Tayside but for the first time finds a resting place within the burgh of Kirriemuir.

Kirrie did win through to the final with Lindsay Brown replacing Cameron McKiddie (on Hol.) & all square at the last end lay shot & guarded. The opposing skip sent the final shot way wide of the brush but wicked off an outlying stone to curl in and remove the lying shot and gain victory

What the Papers Said...

Kirriemuir Herald 5th February 1987

Playing on the day following their Curlers Court, Forfar club can be excused for losing the J.C. Stewart Tankard, which they have held for 11 years. Neil Elder and his rink of Jim Strathearn, Malcolm McBeath and Ian Melrose was responsible for Kirrie's success with a devastating 16-2 win and they needed that winning margin as Mike McVittie's rink of John Gilmour, Jesma Lindsay(sub) and Pat Strathearn(sub) lost 3-13 and Cameron McKiddie's rink of Jim Smith, Jack Donaldson and Alan Bruce were edged out 5 shots to seven.

Kirriemuir Herald 19th February 1987

In Inter-Club competitions Kirrie are enjoying a bonanza year, probably the best ever. Having already won against Panmure, Aberlemno, and Forfar, to their belt they added the scalp of Fothringham when after a gap of 5 years they regained the Ewart-Warden Trophy. >>>
Only Cortachy can now prevent Kirrie completing the Grand Slam when they compete later this month for the Glasswell Cup.

Kirrie did go on to win their match against Cortachy

Kirriemuir Herald 16th April 1987

Kirrie club having already won all their annual inter-club games competitions in one of the best ever years, were delighted to learn this week that they had won Section A of the Dundee Evening League following their promotion from Section B last season.

Kirriemuir Herald 8th October 1987

The annual Bonspiel of Kirriemuir Curling club is a three-rink match for the Stan Milne Trophy and after eight years of trying, Stan Milne finally got his hands on the trophy. Stan had enlisted three lady subs — Alison Strathearn, Isobel Keillor and Cath Arnott. This glamorous team accounted for Dave Torrie's rink of Steven Elder, Colin Smith and Chris Dailly.

Kirriemuir Herald 15th December 1988

In the final of the Forfar Challenge, Cameron McKiddie, Malcolm McBeath, Mike McVittie and John Gilmour met Aberlemno and took an early lead of five shots. Aberlemno replied strongly and led 7-5 after seven ends but the Kirrie rink scored a fine three at the 8th end and the result rested on the last two stones of the ninth and final end. Cameron's last stone was a fine take out, his stone staying in wide on the right of the circle. The last Aberlemno's stone had to remove it and stay in to win the game. The Kirrie stone was duly removed but the Aberlemno one just failed to stick leaving the end blank and Kirrie the winners of an exciting final by eight shots to seven.

Kirriemuir Herald 12th October 1989
Kirriemur had the distinction of playing the first official session at the Forfar Curling Centre. The Club Bonspiel was contested at the fine new facilities and on excellent ice six teams competed for the Stan Milne Trophy. >>> The runaway winner of the first trophy won at the Forfar rink was Neil Elder and his rink of Ian Fraser, Stephen Elder and Alastair Melrose.

Kirriemuir Herald 16th March 1995

If any Kirrie curlers are suffering from amnesia they should forget consulting one particular G.P. – his memory lapse cost him a possible Redhurst final place. Dave Torrie, current holder of the cup and his rink by virtue of turning up, go through to defend the trophy in the final.

Kirriemuir Herald
20th November 1997

The Area 9 Bonspiel at Letham Grange was on Cameron McKiddie's agenda this weekend. In their words, Cameron's rink of Alistair Melrose, Gordon Ager and Colin Smith, all suffering post dance fatigue, started disastrously and were four down after two ends. However a fine draw from Cameron against a lying three stones gave Kirrie a point at the third end. From this point on, the Kirrie men discarded their lethargy and romped home to win 14-4 to take the Area 9 Bonspiel Trophy — for the first time in living memory!

Kirriemuir Herald 4th February 1998

McKiddie Cup time again and three Kirrie rinks faced the same number from Suttieside >>>>>>>>>>>>> However Cameron McKiddie, Jim Strathearn, Mike Strathearn and John Duncan were in top form, both in voice and play. Playing next to them was deafening, the decibels left Suttieside stunned and defeated 18-3.

>>> parts omitted

Kirriemuir Herald 6th April 1995

In good form lately, Jim (Strathearn) had Mark Clark playing lead stones in the Pairs final. With John Gilmour still absent on a memory enhancement course, Neil Elder stepped in again and probably wished he hadn't. On paper it looked a good final, but with George Martin at lead, Neil failed to get off the mark, Jim making no mistakes at all in cruising to a 7-0 win.

Kirriemuir Herald 19th March 1998

A dramatic outcome occurred in the "father versus son" Pairs final last week Mike Strathearn and Jack Kelly whitewashed father Jim Strathearn and John Duncan nine shots to zero, not the close tussle expected. Congratulations go to Mike Strathearn who has been in excellent form all season. Kirriemuir landed a major event on Sunday when Mike McVittie, Mike Strathearn, Bill Martin and Don Sturrock defeated Forfar men to win the Callander Trophy.

Kirriemuir Herald 26th March 1998

Alistair Melrose has ended an excellent season by winning the Forfar Points competition for Kirriemuir. This competition invites all local clubs "Points' winners and runners-up to compete for the local championship.

The Joy of Outdoor Curling

Curling Match between Cortachy & Kirriemuir held on
Loch Heath, Glen Clova, January 2002

Kirriemuir Herald 10th January 2002

Kirriemuir and Cortachy had their own "Grand Match" on Sunday
past at Clova Loch, near the hotel.

For some, this was their first experience of outdoor curling and
they must have been impressed — the sunlit scenery was superb and
the setting in which the loch rests is beautiful. The trophy at
stake was the 'Durston'. It is an annual double rink competition
between the two clubs and ought to be played outdoor when
possible. Few can remember the last time that happened.

Cortachy established an early lead on both sheets. Malcolm
McBeath, Lindsay Brown, Allan Keillor and Allan Thomson kept
working hard and were rewarded with a four at the last end.
However they still finished a shot behind Cortachy, who won
nine- eight. The other rink comprising, Cameron McKiddie, David
Lang, Ian Grubb and Gordon Ager didn't fare too well. They had
no answer to the finely polished stones of Jim and Marnie Ewart.
Cameron's crew lost nine — five.

The outdoor curling is quite a spectacle. Stones are delivered
with considerable force, and in some cases (notably Lindsay
Brown's), the stone's passage resembles the famous bouncing bombs
of Dam-buster fame!

Kirrie President Malcolm McBeath presented the Durston Trophy
to Jim Ewart, Cortachy's winning skip, at the Glen Clova Hotel,
where refreshments were taken.

Members of Cortachy and Kirriemuir Curling Clubs playing for the
Durston Trophy at Loch Heath Glen Clova in January of this year (Kirrie Herald 2002)

Kirriemuir Herald 17th October 2002

Curling Stretches back 460 years

Curling is as much Scotland's national winter sport as indeed whisky is the
national tipple. For centuries, curling has been a favourite game in Scotland and,
in fact, during the first two thirds of the nineteenth century it could be said to
be the Scottish game.

There is little doubt that, with the notary John McQuhin, writing in February 1541
about a challenge between a relative of the abbot and a monk at Paisley Abbey to
throw stones across the ice, the recorded history of curling had begun.

Curlers vied with each other to be closest to the mark on the ice; one part of the
parish played another; trades and occupations played each other; parishes played
against each other.

Early on the cordiality of the game was established. There were no great prizes,
save perhaps for the extraction of dinner and a bowl of toddy from the loser.

It was seen to be a harmless, innocent and healthy amusement and so it has
remained.

Some curling clubs, including most of the Angus Curling province, claim legitimacy
dating back to the middle part of the 19th century.

By 1830 the game had become so popular and widespread that the demand arose for the
founding of the national club to regulate the game.

The Grand Caledonian Curling Club was formed in Edinburgh in 1838, and, while there
were several forms of the game, it opted for the four by two stones format.

In 1843 it became the Royal Caledonian Curling Club, after the Earl of Mansefield
demonstrated the sport to Queen Victoria and Prince Albert on the polished floor
of the ballroom at Scone Palace. The Royal Club promoted the national game by
providing medals for the larger bonspiels that could be arranged by grouping clubs
into 'provinces'.

It also promoted the game abroad and among the cooler countries throughout the
world, twenty associations look to the R.C.C.C. as their mother club.

The R.C.C.C. is also responsible for the 'Grand Match' where, on open-air ice, 2000
curlers meet for the north of Scotland to play the south.

This happened last in 1979 and almost happened at the beginning of this year at
Piper Dam outside Dundee. Six inches of ice are required and unfortunately only five
were achieved.

That same weekend, however, Cortachy Curling Club, one of ten in the Angus Curling
Province, was able to arrange outside ice on Loch Heath in Glen Clova, next to the
Clova Hotel, and is hoping to repeat the experience this winter.

An auld curler's advice to his son

'Hey! faither, there's them a' awa'
Doon to the loch to clean the snaw;
Come 'wa, draw on your buits an gang;
Altho' you're auld, an' no sae strang
As yince ye were, nor yet sae clever,
Ye play as straucht a stane as ever.'
'Na, Davie lad! I'm fairly dune,
Try ye and fill your faither's shoon;
And mind the guid advice I gie ye
When I will no be there to see ye-
And first o' a' aye lift yer stane
Straucht oot ahint ye, while you lean
Your wecht upon your hin'most foot,
The foremost ane aye weel set oot,
To gie ye poo'er and keep ye firm,
And let ye hae full swing o' airm;
And dinna let your back get roun',
But frae the hurdies bend ye doon;
For mind! it's no the souple shoother,
But the firm back that gies the poother.
And when you're playin' keep yer e'e
Aye on your skip, and play where he
Directs ye, even tho' ye'd fain
Whiles play a shottie o' yer ain.
And mind your game maun be attendit
Frae the beginnin' till it's endit;
Nae gawky glowerin' in the air,
But wi' your besom ready there,
And in your place to mind the stane,
To watch and sweep, or leave 't alane.
Ay, faith! the sweepin' o' a rink
Is mair important than some think;
For mony a braw team gets a lickin'
Because the men are unco stickin',
And stand like pailin' posts or slooches,
Wi' buttoned coats and hands in pooches.
Ay laddie! plenty we can name,
Wha played a fair guid curlin' game,
But syne they'll naething do but smoke,
Or glower aboot at aither folk,
Or stand where they should never be
In the skip's road, ahint the tee,

Ay! casting whiles barefaced reflections
Upon his judgement and directions;
But, Davie, ye'll be sure and mind
To tak' nae lesson frae that kind
O' wishy-washy curling graith
Wha save their besoms and their breath
Till the game's ower, and syne they blaw,
Altho' they've gien nae help ava.
And then, whene'er you're asked to play,
You'll aye be ready to obey,
No thinkin' you have been negleckit
Tho' for the first player you're seleckit;
But every stane as carefu' send it
As if on you the game dependit.
Mind you a' this and work your way,
And I've nae doot some future day,
When your apprenticeship's fulfilled,
Ye'll be a skip weel tried and skilled
To fecht and mak' the winnin' score, aye,
As your auld faither did afore ye.
Noo, aff ye go! Enjoy your game!
And when ye're through, mind, come stracht hame,
And dinna stop wi' onybody
To wauger, smoke, and drink at toddy,
Like chaps wha aye maun hae their fill
And curl sae grand atoure a gill,
An' sit and sclore aboot their play,
An' tak up waugers for next day-
Waugers that never do come aff,
For a' their boastin' ends in c'aff.
Ay, laddie! If ye'd aye play straicht,
Ye'll never try your drinking waicht
Alangside o' thae chaps wha curl
A' nicht around the whisky barrel.
Noo, Dave, a present I'm to gie ye-
Tak' my auld favourite stanes doon wi' ye;
Tho' chippit sair, they aye rin soond;
And maybe as the years gang roond
They'll lie as aften near the tee
Wi' you as they hae done wi' me.'   W.

R.C.C.C. Annual 1933-34

Kirriemuir Herald 24th October 2002

A very strong team of Dave Anderson, Malcolm McBeath and John King, skipped by Mike McVittie "were sent hame tae think again" by Kirrie Ladies who achieved a resounding 11- 4 win! " We played the best we could but it was nae use," lamented Mike. "The Ladies were just too good for us!"

Kirriemuir Herald 21st November 2002

Curlers' Court: The highlight of the week had to be the Curlers' Court at which five men, Gordon Elliot, Jim Grant, Malcolm Nicoll, David Lang and Paddy Liddle joined four ladies, Maggie Orr, Kathleen Ager, Angela Watson and Frances Martin in a most harrowing experience during which they saw the light and were admitted to the Fellowship of Curlers.

ADVICE TO YOUNG CURLERS

Auld Scotland ha'ds her heid up high
When curling is the Toast;
That it's the cleanest game on earth
Has aye been her prood boast.

Nae maitter wha's aboot the rink
It's Wullie, Tam or Jock;
We're a' friends there, wha e're is skip,
An' we a' get wer knock.

Yer skips your boss, sae ha'd awa',
An' let him big his heid
As best he can; an' dinna think
That your advice he'll need.

Aye wait on ilka stone that's thrown,
Yes bissom is o' use;
Ye'll ne'er a saft played stane sweep o'er
Gin you're aboot the hoose.

Fit fair, sole clean, wi' eye on cowe,
An dinna fire your shot;
For stanes that come up far o'er fest
Are seldom worth a lot.

Play for your team wi' a' yer micht,
Yer licks ye'll get jist whiles;
Someane a loser's aye to be,
The best ane's he wha smiles.

Up wi' yer heids, gang strecht through life
As ilka curler can:
An gin ye sweep yer ain ice clean
We'll ken we've 'made' a man.

J. HUBERT LOW
R.C.C.C, Annual 1934-35

Kirriemuir Herald
25th November
2004

It must have seemed like a good idea at the time, when Dave Urquhart introduced his son to the intricacies of curling. Dave may now just be having second thoughts, having been comprehensively beaten by his young son (then aged 12) in a recent Group C match. Dave (sen) and Malcolm Nicoll were four shots to the good after two ends. However Dave (jun) ably assisted by skip Allan Keillor, promptly took the next four ends to clinch a six — four victory. Dave (sen) will never hear the end of it!

Kirriemuir Herald
30th March 2006

The winner of the Jim Moffat Trophy, came from the match between Allan Keillor's rink, comprising Mark 'Daffy' Clark, Jon Little & E. Crammond and a bunch of late flowering curlers in the shape of Cameron McKiddie, Gordon Wright, Maggie Orr and Matt Skinner. The game proved to be a tight affair and could have gone either way. Cameron held a slender two shot advantage after six ends. However his team set him up nicely in the next two ends and four shots scored in each end clinched the title for Cameron.

Mark, MD of Grampian Growers grows daffodil bulbs of international quality

A Life Time of Curling

Personal Reflections on the 'Roarin' Game'

Cameron McKiddie

My father, David McKiddie was a keen curler having joined Kirriemuir club in 1930 and he gave sterling service in many capacities, including President during 1950-51. Having moved the family to a house in Glamis in 1953, he finished his days on the ice with Glamis Curling Club. Regretfully I never did see him in action, either at the outdoor 'artificial' rink at Glengate, Kirriemuir or in the indoor rink at Dundee.

My first introduction to the grand game of curling was by Dr Sandy Hardie around 1965 when he persuaded me to come and play for Kirriemuir Rotary Club. This was at the old Dundee Ice rink and at that time, with both feet firmly planted on the crampit, the delivery was rather similar to throwing a bowl as in lawn bowling. No special curling shoes in those days; I favoured a pair of suede shoes, which had seen better days but gave good grip when wielding the brush. I remember being praised for my first outing on the ice but subsequently discovered that many others having their first game almost invariably acquitted themselves amazingly well.

In the 1960's and 70's I recall that evening sessions at Dundee Ice Rink were 5.30pm and 7.45pm, a fairly generous interval and thus it was almost the norm to be able to complete 10 ends before the cessation bell. Then, it was also the rule, that as long as the first lead had started his delivery before the bell, the final end was completed. Crucial matches would therefore see a rush to get on the crampit or hack to beat the bell! This rule was later amended so that if the final stone of the end had come to rest before the bell, a further end was played. I also recall that in those early days there was rarely a full complement of players on the ice, as opposing pairs having delivered their stones would adjourn to the bar for a couple of quick ones, at least once during the game, returning in time to play their stones at the next end. At that time, it was the custom, at Kirriemuir C.C. at least, that beginners started as second and as they improved were promoted to lead. A lead more consistent than that of the opposition lead was considered to give your team an early advantage.

As demand for more ice grew, session times were reduced in length and eventually at Dundee an additional late session at 9.40pm was introduced. As many Kirrie members worked to at least 5.00pm and those in shops to 5.30 or later, the 7.45 session was by far the more convenient and indeed Kirrie settled for several 9.40 sessions in preference to 5.30. It did require a little effort to get out of a comfy chair at 9.00 o'clock to set off for curling but once there all thoughts of time disappeared. Finishing around midnight it was not unusual to return to Kirriemuir in the small hours and sneak into the Ogilvy Arms Hotel for a few nightcaps.

Prior to indoor rinks, curlers relied on Jack Frost to give them ice, which could vary considerably. Curlers also had to contend with stones of varying quality and size and even as they evolved to be of similar weight and size, the running surface, the sole of the stone became more important. These uniform stones of Ailsa Craig or similar granite could be used on the slippy or less slippy side by the simple device of unscrewing the handle and turning the stone over. Stones where the sole had become worn, perhaps from use on outdoor artificial rinks could require an almighty heave to send them up the ice, whereas a stone with a well-polished sole required little effort on all but the dullest of ice. So success in outdoor matches was dependent on the quality of the ice, the quality of the stone and of course the skill of the curler delivering it as instructed.

This inconsistency of stone quality disappeared when

curling for the most part moved indoors to be played with matched uniform stones. However the curler still had to contend with the vagaries of indoor ice, and the ability of the skip to read the ice early in the game and adjust the direction accordingly was a skill on its own. The old Dundee Ice Rink and no doubt others, with odd quirks and falls, could be quite a challenge. Kirrie members, the late Bruce Paul and Jim Smith, great readers of the ice would often give negative hand if required, a ploy used to great success.

Without doubt the greatest change in curling took place, when during the late 1960's, early 70's the old crampit was gradually replaced with the modern day hack and the sliding delivery arrived. I recall the idea came from Canada and one of the earliest curlers in this area to master the technique was David Patullo of Forfar Curling Club. He became such a formidable opponent that others were quick to follow his example. However in order to perfect the slide, purposely designed curling shoes with a slippy sole were essential so it was goodbye to the old baffies and the like.

This sliding delivery was not easily mastered and thus sprung up practice sessions, where coaches taught novices and experienced curlers alike this new form of delivery. While the old hands brought up to curl from the crampit, at times struggled to adapt, novice curlers, properly taught would sooner reach a curling ability that was ever possible in days gone by.

The Hog line, drawn across the ice some 12 feet from the hack, had previously had but one use – stones played which did not clear the far hog line were removed from play. Now it had a second use – stones had to be released from the delivery before reaching the near hog line. How opposing players would gather at the hog line to ensure the release was made in time!

So curling had now reached a stage when stones were uniform; delivery, albeit with many variations, became more accurate leaving just the ice as a variable factor. Soon however, new purpose made rinks employing skilled ice masters with the right equipment were able to produce ice of uniform consistency and even able to adjust the speed of the ice to suit the level of competition.

The strike or knockout game could now be played with devastating accuracy, threatening not only the joy of curling and its multitude of skills, but putting its very future in jeopardy.

A famous or infamous game was recorded at Aviemore in the 1970's, when the great curler Chuck Hay (Men's World Champion 1967), won his 10-end match by one shot to zero! Something had to be done and done quickly or curling would quickly lose all appeal to curlers and spectators alike.

Following some preliminary trials and experiments the **free guard zone** was introduced in 1990, whereby stones lying between the hog line and the house could not be removed from play by either of the leads. This rule had an immediate effect on the appeal and tactics of the game and the future of curling was secured.

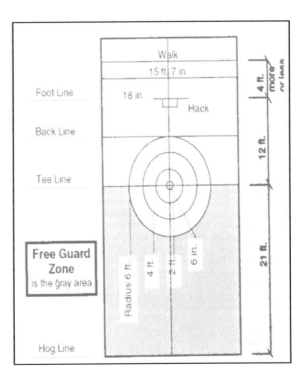

Increasingly in almost all sports as skill and competition became even keener so too has attention been paid to developing sportswear and equipment to the optimum level.

The well-dressed curler may have all or some of the following:

Cap, beret or-other headgear	For warmth & decoration but there has been the suggestion that protective headgear be worn to lesson the chance of a head injury in a fall. We can sometimes be too mollycoddled and in over 40 years, I have seen many curlers fall on the ice but I think a broken wrist or arm is about as bad as I have witnessed.
Jersey, fleece,– body warmer	Very often incorporating the curler's name along with the name and crest of their curling club.
Stretch trousers-	To give freedom during delivery.
Curling shoes-	The lead shoe having a special slippy sole to aid the slide during delivery.
Kipper –	To slip over the shoe with the slippy sole to give better grip on the ice while sweeping.
Glove(s) –	To protect the ice surface from being marked by the bare hands.
Brush –	The old besom or broom has all but disappeared from most rinks and even the bristle brush is fast being replaced with a pad of a variety of artificial material, which cleans and lasts better.
Stop Watch –	Favoured by those at the top of the game so that the speed of the ice can be quickly be Assessed.
Crutch -	Used by some to steady their delivery.
Stick –	For those unable to bend sufficiently to deliver the stone, this device allows them to deliver from an upright position and so continue to enjoy their sport.
Curling Bag -	An essential item considering the gear & equipment mentioned above!

The Future of Curling

Reports from the Royal Caledonian Curling Club do not make easy reading. The last decade or two has seen the closure of several curling rinks, the demise of many curling clubs and a worrying reduction in the number of participants. Some of the older rinks built in the 30's and 40's were past their sell-by date, too expensive to run and maintain and simply no longer sustainable. Even some built within the last 20 years have also closed. Few companies or individuals would rush to invest in a curling rink where returns on the investment are so uncertain. Certainly some of the newer rinks were designed to be much more efficient, better-insulated and requiring less maintenance. However all rinks have seen the cost of power increase dramatically and there is a limit by which ice charges can be increased. Perhaps there is a need for more local authorities to support the establishment of well-designed efficient sustainable rinks.

So while the loss of some curling rinks could explain some reduction in the number of curlers there are many other factors to consider. In the past, a sizeable proportion of the curling stalwarts came from the farming fraternity who, during the winter months had the time to devote to their favoured pastime. Farmers and their wives accounted for a sizeable proportion of curlers able to play during the day. However, many lean years in agriculture through the 80's onwards, drastically reduced the numbers playing during the day, this loss of revenue felt by many rinks. The current worldwide economic downturn, we are told, will take a long time to recover, so there will be less money about, some economies are inevitable and we are likely to see further loss in the number of curlers.

However as an eternal optimist I am certain that the game we love so much will continue.

Yes, when funds are available we need more investment in well designed, super efficient curling rinks, financed partly by local or national government if private investors are not forthcoming. Clubs must continue to encourage the youth to take up the game by whatever means are appropriate.

Rhona Martin's triumph of securing gold at the Winter Olympics in Salt Lake City in 2002 gave huge publicity to the game, her final fantastic shot to take the championship thrilling viewers the world over.

Maybe, as some believe, our present global warming is cyclical – certainly when reading old minutes about curling clubs, there were frequent reports in the past of the non appearance of Jack Frost, sometimes for years at a time. Perhaps if our climate is indeed cyclical, a cold period is on the cards and curling may go back to its very roots to be played outdoors. Then future generations of curlers may again thrill to the echoing sound of the roar of the stone as it thunders it way across the ice.

Epitaph
And when the Great Scorer comes
To write against your name,
He writes not that you won or lost–
But how you played the game.

Curlers' Grace

O Lord wha's love surrounds us a'
And brings us a' thegither;
Wha' writes your laws upon oor hearts,
And bids us help each ither.

We bless Thee for Thy bounties great,
For meat and hame and gear;
We thank Thee, Lord, for snaw and ice -
But still we ask for mair.

Gi'e us a hert to dae whit's richt,
Like curlers true and keen;
To be guid friends along life's road,
And soop oor slide aye clean.

O Power abune whose bounty free,
Oor needs and wants suffices;
We render thanks for Barley Bree,
And meat that appetises.

Be Thou our Skip throughout life's game,
An' syne we're sure to win;
Tho' slow the shot and wide the aim,
We'll soop each ither in.

Rev. David Dick B.D.

Usually only the first 3 verses of this grace are said - Ed

The officials are recorded below in honour of the service given to Kirriemuir Curling Club.

Officials of Kirriemuir Curling Club 1809 - 2009

Presidents		Secretaries		Treasurers	
1809 – 54	Unknown*	1809 – 54	Unknown	1854 – 54	Unknown
1855	William Osler	1855 – 70	Robert Forrest	1855 – 70	Robert Forrest
1856 – 69	James Forrest	1871	William Grant. Grant	1871	William Grant
1870 – 93	Col. Grant of Logie	1872 – 75	John Mustard	1872 – 75	John Mustard
1894 – 17	General Kinloch	1876 – 79	Alexander Watson	1876 – 82	Alexander Watson
1918 – 19	Lord Lyell	1880 – 92	David Savege	1883 – 11	Stewart Lindsay
1920 – 28	P.G. Duncan	1893	James Forrest	1912 – 25	Thomas Leslie
1929 – 30	David Savege	1894 – 05	David Savege	1926 – 28	Stewart McKenzie
1931 – 36	J.A. Carnegie	1906 – 17	J.A. Carnegie	1929 – 34	James Wedderspoon
1937 – 38	J.C. Stewart	1918 – 28	John Scott	1935 – joint	B.G. Carnegie
1945	Charles Lyon	1929 – 34	James Wedderspoon	1945 holders	James Wedderspoon
1946 – 47	James R. Annand	1935 –	joint B.G. Carnegie	1946 – 49	T.J. Kennedy
1948 – 49	James Wedderspoon	1945	holders James Wedderspoon	1950 – 65	J.K. Beattie
1950 – 51	David McKiddie**	1946 – 49	T.J. Kennedy	1966 – 78	J.M. Moffat
1952 – 54	B.G. Carnegie	1950 – 65	J.K. Beattie	1979 – 81	Iain Grubb
1955 – 56	H.G. Douglas	1966 – 78	J.M. Moffat	1982 – 84	Tom Steel
1957	E.K.Durston	1979 – 86	Cameron McKiddie	1985 – 93	Chris Dailly
1958	H.G. Douglas	1987 – 96	Malcolm McBeath	1994 – 04	Bill Martin
1959 – 60	Eric Brown	1997 – 01	Bill Keillor	2005 –	Ewan Cameron
1961 – 62	G. Wallace Neilson	2002 – 04	Jim Miller		
1963 – 64	William S. Lees	2005 – 06	Gordon Wright		
1965	James R. Arnott	2007 –	David Urquhart		
1966 – 67	James Smith				
1968 – 69	Ian Ewart				
1970 – 71	A.B. Paul				
1972 – 73	William Mills				
1974 – 75	Cameron McKiddie**				
1976 – 77	W.S.Upton				
1978 – 79	Jack Donaldson				
1980 – 81	Lindsay Brown				
1982 – 83	John Gilmour				
1984 – 85	David Torrie				
1986 – 87	James Strathearn				
1988 – 89	Dudley Dorman				
1990 – 91	Neil Elder				
1992 – 93	Iain Melrose***				
1994 – 95	Bill Keillor				
1996 – 97	Ewan Cameron				
1998 – 99	Russell Hamilton				
2000 – 01	Malcolm McBeath				
2002 – 03	Alistair Melrose***				
2004 – 05	Alan Keillor				
2006 – 07	John King				
2008 – 09	Cameron McKiddie				

*   Unfortunately there are no surviving records from this period

**   Father & son

***   Father & son

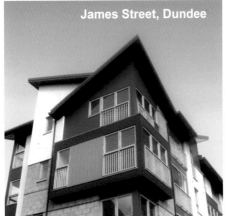
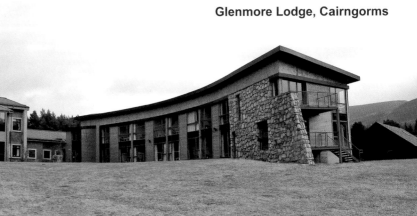